AN ALPHABET OF BIRDS

≈≈≈-☼-≈≈≈

AN ALPHABET OF BIRDS

TOTI O'BRIEN

≈≈≈-☼-≈≈≈

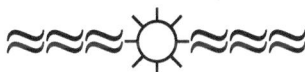

MOONRISE PRESS

Copyright Information

An Alphabet of Birds by Toti O'Brien

This book is published by Moonrise Press
P.O. Box 4288, Los Angeles – Sunland, CA 91041-4288,
www.moonrisepress.com; info@moonrisepress.com

Manufactured in the United States of America

The Library of Congress Publication Data
O'Brien, Toti, (b. 1959)
[Title] An Alphabet of Birds (in English)
184 pages (viii pp. + 176 pp.) 15.2 cm x 22.9 cm.
Written in English.

.

ISBN 978-1-945938-41-2 (paperback)
ISBN 978-1-945938-42-9 (eBook in ePub format)

10 9 8 7 6 5 4 3 2 1

TABLE OF CONTENTS

≈≈≈☼≈≈≈

ACKNOWLEDGMENTS

These stories, or earlier versions of them, appeared in the
following publications:

*82: 'In the Moonlight'
Animal, A Beast of a Magazine: 'Pavo Regina'
Beauty in Unexpected Places, an anthology: 'Beautiful Bones'
Cloud Women: 'Spectrum,' 'Lunacy,' 'The Volvo and the Bike'
Communion: 'September'
Dragon Poetry: 'Precious'
Edgard Allan Poet: 'The Leaf and the Butterfly,' 'Sunset Walk'
Entropy: 'Doves'
Folio: 'November'
Indiana Voice: 'The Salmon and the Bear'
Litro NY: 'The Staircase'
Little Somethings: 'Gardener's Companion'
Lost Coast: 'The Statue'
Microfiction: 'Peacocks'
Mojave Review: 'Speculum'
Mortar: 'Terrafirma'
River's Poets: 'In the Garden'
Rooted, an anthology: 'The Decadence of Grapefruit'
Ruminate: 'At Risk'
Sein und Werden: 'The Lawn'
Seven Circles: 'Five Senses'
Spectrum: 'Milagros'
The Linnet's Wings: 'The Fountain'
The Magnolia Review: 'Dog Days'
Unearthed: 'Engraved'
Wilderness House: 'Part Out'

AN ALPHABET OF BIRDS

IN THE MOONLIGHT

He saw her silhouette, dark, against the whitewashed walls. Hands in front of her face, as if she were praying.

He came close and took the frog from her hands.

"Stop kissing it," he said. "He'll never become a prince."

She didn't believe him.

≈≈≈☼≈≈≈

THE LAWN

I have counted the animals. They are ten if I leave out a pair of silhouettes hiding under the porch, quasi invisible from the street. Not that the other ten truly jumped at me. It took time to acknowledge them, although they are in the open, scattered across the expanse of an impeccable lawn.

Technically I should be able to see them at once, if I find the best vantage point. But I am fiddling with perspective and distance in vain. Maybe a narrative kink? See, these folks seem to be part of different stories. I have to turn the page, so to speak, each time that my gaze...

Wait, I am wrong. They belong together, I am sure. For a start, they have the same age! Look at the coat of verdigris spread over their surface. Isn't it quite uniform? They are all green, and steadily so. On a green lawn, which is part of the strange fascination they exude.

But their tone, so similar to the shade of the vegetation, doesn't truly blend in. I see why... Those puppies are old, while the grass intimately flirting with them is young, vibrant, fresh. The grass shines under the sun, while the animals are dusty, passé.

Yes. As soon as I notice the discrepancy, I decipher the unease I previously felt. I realize what my mind initially couldn't grasp. These are ghosts. Solid, and quite heavy, but ghosts.

They are bizarrely staggered, askew…

It is hard to understand why they would be arranged in such fashion, if not following a kind of perverse design. They are disposed on diagonals that don't intersect, offset, escaping, tangential. The result is one of subtle disquiet in a formally bucolic tableau.

Why? That is quite obvious. No one sees anyone. Oh, no, they aren't blind… They have eyes, as green as the rest. They are neither asleep nor daydreaming, as their tense necks and pointed ears prove. Alertness is nearly overstated, with a somehow pleasant effect, a sense of immediacy not usually granted with ghosts.

These are solid, I said. They are lively, too. But they look away.

The large rabbit is turned towards the house. The small ones on the left, round and cute, capriole on all four while their mom or dad, I can't tell, proudly stands on hind legs.

Mom or Dad has a broken ear, still attached but exposing a pale chalky core, like a torn cactus leaf. There's something about it… sad, almost indecent and yet, like all scars, the bent ear lends an aura of authority to its owner. He or she who proudly wears it, I'm sure, was wounded in action. There's a glorious past, close at reach, a legacy to be proud of.

But the bunnies below don't know the first thing about it.

While the rabbits look at the house, a couple of piglets (peering out of a bush of scarlet hibiscus) aim at a nondescript pole of the fence.

The two are slightly diverging, as if starting off for a same errand and then briskly but irrevocably deciding to part. One seems mesmerized by a hidden, mysterious something very lowly located. Did it spot a hole in the dirt, containing a treasure? The rusted lid of a trunk, just unburied by an industrious mole? The intensity of its gaze confirms such hypothesis.

But its brother, or cousin, doesn't show the faintest curiosity for what lies underground. Oh, no. Its snout is pointed upwards, as if wishing to catch the last flash of color from a disappearing balloon, or else counting crows.

The duck, next to the left, bluntly ignores the piglets. Well, it could at least glance at the rabbit, and immediately grasp how much they are alike. Rather specular. They both stand alert, valiant, tense, by a pair of frolicking youth that couldn't care less.

With a drop, with an iota of common sense the duck wouldn't only notice the rabbit, but it would befriend it, start a conversation, why not? It stares at the garage door instead, impassive, indifferent even to the branch of a Joshua tree mischievously tickling its butt.

On the piglets' right, in the shadow, trying to make itself inconspicuous, a goose scans a tree trunk, closely surveying the progression of a long line of ants. Not a single detour, not the shortest smoke break will escape its watch and, I bet, its fiery rebuke.

On the right of this aloof loner, a single chick fell. Almost. It leans on a side, as if stuck between heaven and hell. Its slant body mirrors the rabbit's ripped ear across an ideal (but sloppily drawn) diamond shape. The poor thing must have kept its awkward posture for ages… Its stern dad is frankly unconcerned.

From the tree our goose keenly scrutinizes, a robot is hanging.

I haven't counted it among the beasts. I am counting it now. Eleven, that is. It is handsome, assembled with miscellaneous tin cans. Ten tin cans, correct.

I am not fooled by the naivety of its design. In fact, I can't stop admiring it, knowing how hard is to achieve true simplicity. Here's a small masterpiece! Not only its shape skirts perfection, also its color amazes me. What was silvery at first worked itself, past rust, to a rich chocolate brown. Metal morphed into bark, wood, perhaps terracotta.

The robot isn't a phantom. No way… its very countenance proves it. Bottle caps form its eyes and then something else, nose or mouth. Hard to say, but the resulting frown is so ineffable, it miraculously becomes wise. Understanding, sympathetic, compassionate.

From its high vantage point, backed up by the authority of the tree, fastened to its mighty branch, the robot swings in the breeze. Barely, and yet sufficiently. Meaning, it enjoys a margin of flexibility cruelly denied to the ghost animals it has under control. Or, let's say, gracious supervision.

Unlike me, the robot can see them all simultaneously, helped by a delicate oscillation, slightly turning to the left, to the right...

Sometimes it looks my way. And it smiles.

≈≈≈☼≈≈≈

THE STAIRCASE

It stuck out in a corner of the park.

Of what once was a park, now disheveled like an old beauty in rags, gravel disorderly mixed with dirt, scrawny boxwood hedges. A few pine trees, still handsome, still claiming some pride, spread their prickly needles around, adding to the dusty feeling, the untidiness.

It stuck out, the stub of concrete, bulky and wide. Getting close, you would see that it was a spiral. You would notice the wall that started in the center and then turned around, as it rose, like a roll of licorice.

Long before, it must have been a staircase. Only one side remained and no steps at all. Just a ridge, like the backbone of a huge, coiled beast... Mammoth, dragon, dinosaur, you could almost see it get up, suddenly or in slow motion, shaking away ashes of time. Could such thing occur?

Judging by the ambient creepiness, it could. A tall fence erased all street sounds, also blocking the view and severing the villa from the surrounding townscape. The wrecked mansion hung in midair, so to speak, together with its ghost gardens. Remote, quiet. Suspended. Nowhere.

There, our troop had its quarters. Having seized the estate from some careless scion, the town rented it out for a trifle, but expected in return a tolerant attitude about maintenance and repairs.

Fine. The company manager didn't mind. Tell the truth, he had guessed that the very decadence of the grounds added value to them, made the deal more profitable. Let me explain.

Our troop specialized in stilts, acrobatics and physical stunts. The park, with its raised platforms, empty pools, half grottos, crumbling gazebos, all incongruous, truncated residual of bygone architectures, was a marvelous playground. An ideal gymnasium, waiting to be filled with tumblers and fools in order to come alive. And then time would resume its flow, death relent its grip, at least take a break.

Our new members, freshly hired, were trained outdoors through a variety of drills. The stub hosted one of those. Which one? As a general rule, no explanations were ever provided beforehand. Surprise, yes, was part of the challenge.

An instructor demonstrated the routine and the newbies, in turns, replicated it. That's all. Either I demonstrated or I watched, taking notes for later discussion. In such case, I tried to be very accurate.

To no avail, I confess. My eye was diverted, each time, by a technically irrelevant bit that stole all my attention... the split second, the flash when people's face changed. God, how fast it occurred! It was hard to seize the hairline crack, as thin as its effect was spectacular. But I craved it, because folks were transfigured, yes. Only once. Then, they became used. Then they knew. That's how we could fool the trainees.

Sure. We could predict and prevent the shift of our countenance. Drop? Drop is what best defines the phenomenon, if still metaphorically. Of course we didn't pick up ears, cheeks, chins from the ground, but during that ineffable moment features got longer. One inch? More? I believe all muscles let go, joints releasing in concert.

As I said, looks were metamorphosed. Personality clues were wiped off, completely erased. In a blink people lost all character inscribed on their mugs, and whatever past, luggage, memory they had carried along.

Suddenly, they blanked out. They became generic, unnamed. Simplified, stripped down to the core. Their traits pure, non-descript, a few dots, few lines, what a kindergartener could draw.

Is it how we look during orgasm? Or when we see death? When else do we look that way? I couldn't help wondering.

People got ahold of themselves. When, a minute later, they finished, they wore their usual heads.

Wait. I can tell you when and why the shift happened, drawing from my own experience. Right, I had my first time and I recall my feelings, though I did not see myself. I do not regret it. I suppose that's a part of me I don't care to acknowledge. Or to picture, at least.

The shift happens because of the absence of steps. That is the only cause. You are asked to run up the wall, that one spike, that bestial backbone. It's not high, so no one is scared. You just climb, feet aligned as if on a tightrope, a comfortable one, wide enough to allow the average sole. You boldly proceed as the teacher previously did. And it catches you by surprise. The end, I mean.

Since no steps are there, you can't say, "three, two... one more step and I'll pull the brakes." You can't truly gauge distances. All is fluid and all goes too fast. You are propelled, your body inclined to gain forward momentum, easing the ascending effort. The end briskly leaks in and ruptures the whole. It explodes the continuum, like a treacherous gunshot out of nowhere.

It's not fear striking, but a kind of extreme, oversized awareness. Your brain discerns emptiness just a microsecond too late. As it tries to alert the body, it finds it off guard and your stomach, on the spot, sinks into your heels. Your face... it's not fear...

All first timers react in similar fashion if with slight variations. Someone freezes. Some decelerate, hesitate. Some take a few more steps or just one, in slow motion, after a sudden stop. Someone shakes. All turn back, of course. Not too gracefully. No, not even those who push nearest to the chasm do it artfully, displaying mastery and savoir-faire.

The first time they all encounter a monster of sorts. I haven't found its name yet.

But I know it doesn't only dwell within the old staircase, which has probably crumbled as I write. No. The monster that snaps away our disguise and shows our bared soul must have other hides, and I'd like to find them.

Why? Didn't I say?

Because of the ravishing, incomparable beauty of the anonymous stares. Calm. All claim, all anxiety, all greed vanished. At peace as the dead is, but fiercely alive. No, those awed, wide-open eyes aren't empty. They are wells of infinity. They contain all that was ever seen, whatever you'd need or want, although...

Truly, right then nothing is wanted, neither by the stunned wall riders, nor by the by-stander who drinks in eternity, looking up at those awkward angels.

Awkward, wingless and suddenly aware of such lack. Angels, still.

≈≈≈☼≈≈≈

THE LEAF AND THE BUTTERFLY

The dilemma of the leaf and the butterfly lasted for the whole summer, a dry, unusually hot season causing plants to parch, pale and languidly undress.

I believe it started with a leaf, yellow and relatively small, perhaps from a linden tree? Crossing from right to left in front of my windshield, obviously on a descendant curve because it was falling.

Slowly. So slowly and so randomly that I erroneously took it for a butterfly, noticing my mistake only at the last moment… Oh, no! It is a leaf!

That's the crux where my mind got nailed.

As I said, the dilemma occupied me for the entire season. Day after day, I kept marveling at a confusion of falling leaves and fluttering butterflies, also very frequent a sight. Yellow and yellow, about the same size.

It was hard not to be cheated by that superimposing, that double entendre… What's a butterfly, geometrically speaking, but a leaf with a crease in the middle? They are two stages of a same origami, correct? A crease there, along the leaf's rib… not that difficult, truly. Then you fold it, simply following the mark. You press down with your thumbnail and it just takes flight. The trick is complete.

That must be why, as much as I tried to tell the difference, I couldn't. Both the foliage and the insects kept fooling me. Did they know? I doubt it.

Was any sensibility offended, was the order of things

even altered if I missed, more than once but with perfect honesty, the identity of those aerial interferences? That I really wanted to know, that perplexed me.

Let me come to the point that truly irritated my consciousness, like a needle pricking my thumb. Was there proof that a leaf was a leaf and a butterfly a butterfly, if I happened to believe the opposite? Wasn't it a mere case of definition? Aren't insects insects because some of us so decided? Isn't it the same for plant parts? If no one were witnessing, would nomenclature matter at all?

Could I merrily call leaves flies and flies leaves, indeed, or petals, or candy wraps, being somehow totally right in my blur? Who was going to claim imprecision? Was there any, if nobody complained?

Clearly, I was debating within myself philosophical matters of the simplest level, trite arguments on the respective values of language, perception and essence, turned inside out for a million of times since the Greek. But, perhaps due to the brain-splitting heat of that pitiless summer, I was losing my mind, in fact, at a steady pace.

Other questions started urging me, spontaneous, unwanted, following each other in waterfall style. How long does an insect live? How longer is that than a leaf's descending parabola? Couple of days versus couple of minutes. Does it make a substantial difference? Not considering that a dead leaf can resuscitate, blown up by a sudden whirlpool, even long after it reached the end of its journey…

Has the fact that butterflies independently move and leaves don't any relevance? I admit it does. It is easier to pick up a leaf than to catch a butterfly. Although, truly, I have seen five-year-olds pin down whole collections of winged creatures, and I have hopelessly run after a twig or petal puffed away by capricious winds whenever my hand came close. Just a matter of chance.

Was my musing trying to smooth out disparities, then? Create a broad, generous category unifying fauna and flora, hence dissolving my doubts? I guess so.

Ultimately the question came down to god, and a leftover bucket of yellow paint. Plus a stack of cheap paper squares…

Nothing to be thrilled about. A rainy afternoon. Gloomy, at that. He/she started with a simple model. Passive. Pendulous. A little flaccid perhaps, but capable of true abandon. Then, as I said, god folded it on the centerline, slightly pinching for aerodynamics sake. And the stem became antennae. And a tiny, rudimentary engine (just a thought in the creator's mind) added some curves and some freedom to the still erratic trajectory.

A brush stroke with that flashy color, that cocktail of lemon and straw, transparent and tangy, then the entire bulk was kicked down on Earth, where it still orbits.

While the almighty still folds, more sophisticated models, correct? God makes things multicolored now, unmistakable, things that know what they are or so they believe, things that want to be called by their name.

≈≈≈☼≈≈≈

DARWIN

Those who blurted such absurdity (as the elders defined it) are the same who carry their picnic far into the woods rather than perusing the neat, perfect areas safely located at the edges.

Seeking wilderness is fine, of course. No one would think of stopping you. We are a tolerant kind. Rules? Of course, but not too many or too sticky. There is no objection to personal choice when it comes to leisurely destinations. Only, as we know, what you do describes you... The small clique officially eager for adventure, substantially enamored with, shall I say, elusiveness, doubtlessly exhibits a tad of snobbery.

Who cares? Here's the point. Once, they claimed they had seen flying birds, and they sounded sincere. Then they said it again. Then, again.

Sure, we know nothing stays the same. Things change, which means mutations occur. Very slowly, and yet they must start somewhere, at a moment in time. Here and now, for instance. Though, mutations always respond to some type of logic, have a meaning, correct? And why should birds fly? Such an extraneous skill for them and so attuned, instead, to the proper flying creatures. Fish! Not only for the most obvious reason, which is the homogeneity of the two habitats fish peruse, seas and skies, tinted of a same color...

One could object air isn't blue. Technically, it has no color. Well, water has none either. Technically, I mean if you pull it apart. But you don't, and everything looks equally and unbreakably azure, a flush, smooth continuum. Besides the horizon, sure, but that's a thin line.

Anyway, habitat isn't truly the point. Species is, its adapted morphology, carefully evolved traits. What could be more blatantly aerodynamic than fish, compact, slender, slick, a vector made for propulsion and speed?

While, as we can easily observe in our backyards, in the orchards and fields, anywhere, birds are made for hopping. And for poking holes with their beaks, hiding nuts and seeds with compulsive frenzy, racing with gangs of squirrels equally crazed by such single-minded passion.

Birds, like squirrels, are also zealous builders of nests, an activity they pursue with extreme alacrity. They lay eggs, produce progeny and feed them, steadily perpetuating the hole-digger, nut-storer crowd. They take countless baths, gingerly preening their feathers... A superfluous garb, residual of old, obscure, obsolete body structures, once they must have been precious if instinct still prompts such assiduous care.

Well, imagine! The far-picnic-goers said that is what birds use. Yes, for flying! Their wings! Feathers? Why, if fins are such a perfect mechanism, swinging lightly in the breeze, folded and unfolded by wind, offering no resistance, no friction? Why should nature ever turn itself to those baroque origami, labyrinths of frail bone and cartilage, strange collapsible mazes? For sure, it would take elbow grease to efficiently operate them. Can a bird, only trained for drilling, knitting, weaving, brushing itself clean—very circumscribed occupations—suddenly afford such athleticism?

It can't for a crucial reason, a deal-breaker. Such a feat would take lots of oxygen, and birds talk too much. In fact, they never stop. That is why fish fly, dear, fish only. Because they shut up. It is in their nature, I know. They couldn't talk if they wanted to. But I'm sure they don't feel that need, why would they? Look at the life they lead! Always traveling. Unbound. Up. Or down. Rise. Dive. To the right and left. Spirals, circles and figure eights. Eternity. Dance. Fish dance, they do. They are busy and content. Questions, comments?

Flying, like swimming, is a quintessentially quiet form of art, to be practiced just like meditation, in silence. Can't be done otherwise.

Some say birds sing. Well, they rather chat. Chatter, yes! Have animate and articulate conversations. Some say their intense vocalism is related to their digging, to those geometries of nuts buried in dirt. Do they count them? Perhaps. Do they recite coordinates, as if playing a huge, endless Battleship? The elders claim we have learned language from them… the passing by of information, all this cozy, familiar, perpetual din.

As they make so much noise and with such gusto, birds, like us, cannot leave the ground.

But since the wild-picnic-eaters dared to associate the words "bird" and "fly," confusion has joined our lot. At least doubt that things might change or be about to, embracing some unsettling paradox.

And we will accept it, of course. I said we are a tolerant bunch. No hard rule, at least not consistently enforced. Birds especially do whatever they want. We never intrude. We don't speak the same language. Perhaps a derivation.

Only, I wonder, if there is proof to the rumor, if the myth is confirmed as reality…

If these birds, and those, overtime should truly learn how to fly, either mimicking fish (the incommensurable gap between feather and fin notwithstanding) or by trial and error, wild experimentation or divine inspiration, will they take off and leave? All of them?

Even more, I ask myself or whoever would please oblige with an answer…

Will they ever return?

≈≈≈☼≈≈≈

PAVO REGINA

Busy fixing, then emptying the house that I have listed for sale, overwhelmed by chaos, un-domesticity, un-coziness, for the last few months I have given up gardening. Quite regretfully, as the sight of my small plot invaded by wilderness doesn't improve my mood.

And yet thanks to their careless status, to the sloppiness so depressing me, you have found the grounds perfectly fit. "What a tasteful haven," you have thought, "discreet, intimate, safe." Were you feeling tired? I guess. At the end of your brooding month you'll be completely exhausted. You have melted among the tall grass, spreading yourself like a puddle, plumage color of mud, dust, dry leaves, with a shimmer of blue reminding of water.

Oh no, I didn't see you arrive. I almost bumped on you the other night, in the semi-dark. You blended within the landscape like a rock, a root, or a trunk... But you were alive, and I gasped.

Alive, and yet so quiet that you seemed to have left the animal realm, making yourself as vegetal, as mineral as you possibly could. Camouflage... what's the gist of it? Lose identity and espouse similarity. Smudge contours and blur edges in order to vanish. Your feathers the color of dirt, your breath imperceptible. Sphinx-like head, vitreous eyes.

Though, as I neared, moved around, backed away, you followed me with your gaze and your long, thin neck slightly twitched. But the bulk of your body stood still. If you were afraid you perfectly knew how to conceal it.

You were spread like a puddle, I said, a small oval pond. But you were also compact, collected. Anchored. Voluntarily shackled. In chains.

I have seen the same uncanny calmness before, emanating from a bird at the other end of the spectrum, as small as you are huge. Tiny, tiny hummingbird, also sitting on eggs and stone-still. How could that frantic being transform into an icon, marvelously immobile or rather unmovable? As you are, night and day.

Monday, a raging storm has exploded and I have worried about you. I don't have an umbrella... Here the weather is sunny and dry. Monday, though, a storm has broken and I have asked myself how you'd cope. I had seen your eggs once... I mean partially, hardly a peek when you slightly lifted on your toes as if to stretch your spine. I had counted five, but I knew there could be more. They are humongous. No way you could possibly move them.

You have remained in place with no visible sign of trouble. All of your vital sap must have spiraled inwards, helping you to endure the chill, the discomfort, just as for a homeless girl coiling in a corner, curled to keep her viscera, her lungs, her heart warm. Head down, face on her knees, breathing slowly, yet unable to control her shivers. Waiting for the rain to stop, sooner or later.

Did you know that the rain would cease? I don't think so. Did you know what the thing that pelleted you was? Come on. I am applying the wrong lexicon. All you knew was that you should stay put, belly glued against the bumpy stones you had laid and would shield, now, against all adversities.

Is this motherly love? What I witnessed, truly, was a quiet bird sitting on eggs under the downpour.

It would pass. The storm. Did your instinct tell you? Not sure. What instinct requires from you is blind, timeless endurance... Patience without clocks or calendars becomes infinite. Quintessential, because unconditional.

What would you do, I muse, in case of a hurricane? An earthquake? Would you die like a soldier on the front line? A sentry at her post? Would you run, let's say, if a coyote were around? Or a couple of hawks?

Last week I have told Mother about you. Well, I have written, as her hearing is poor and she doesn't pick up the phone. Also her memory is gone, so the things I write do not register. They just disappear, but I thought your story might please her for a minute. There's a brooding peahen, Mom, in my front yard...

I couldn't have guessed that she would remember days later, send a delayed response. "The hen makes me feel jealous." That sounded sibylline... Why would Mom, such a lady, envy a bird stuck in dirt, rain or sunshine? Frail, exposed, underfed, too warm or too cold? Sitting on five boulders?

Then it dawned on me. Mom envied the hen because she was sitting, indeed. And the eggs hadn't hatched, and the progeny was as stuck as the parent was, safe, under control. Mom envied the bird whose nest, so to speak, was still full. The bird who had lost nothing.

First my son, more practical than I am, has started feeding you. I had trusted that you'd provide for yourself, your long neck pecking at the surrounding grass. And you do, though I have learned that after your brooding month you will be entirely depleted.

My son brought you a dishful of oats. When we found it empty, it was hard to tell if you had eaten or else disdainfully spilled the grains. Hard to say, because you never budge in our presence and the messy grounds would hide leftovers from sight. But as further inquiry has proved you ate, slowly and secretly. I have sifted those weeds, darling. There's no trace of food.

Now you let me approach, and I am feeding you. Your eye sticks on me like a magnet but your neck doesn't twitch, which is quite a change. Your neck is tense, alert, an antenna. It betrays what your eyes, as glassy and reflective as if you sported sunshades, do not. But I see depth behind your shiny corneas, a dark camera of sorts... You are on guard.

Still, your neck doesn't spasm anymore to track my every gesture. You have relaxed a bit in my presence, which fills me with joy. I appreciate being trusted by the animal kind, birds especially. They only trust when they know that you will not harm them, and such knowledge is usually sound.

The hen knows I am not threatening and I didn't have to talk, sell, bargain my way into her confidence. Didn't have to befriend her in words, not even in facts... I believe it's neither the food I provide that loosened her armor, nor the reiteration of my innocuous visits, the buildup of my tameness, at least not entirely. I believe she bases her assumption upon something more intimate, a transuding of hormones, perhaps pheromones. Perhaps something olfactive, a smell.

Well, the hen assumes nothing. Her hormones have adjusted to my bodily script, that is all. Less adrenaline storms throughout her than it did before, maybe, when I linger on my messy front lawn.

All the same, her serenity is a badge of honor, making me feel less... evil? Less dangerous than I, we are by nature, I mean inadvertently, unconsciously... we, the people, yes.

Am I hearing a mowing sound? It must be my neighbor. It is early and I am still in bed but the noise comes closer, obnoxious. Wait! The freaking sound is right in my front yard. Quick! Get dressed, get out, see what happens!

My front yard has grown so Amazonian that the guy next door could take it no more. He has decided to give it a complimentary haircut. It's a gift, therefore he doesn't ask for permission. It's a present, so I need to be delicate.

I explain that I'm moving. I am emptying and repairing the house, hence I didn't have a minute to spare for gardening chores. Cleaning my front lawn is also on my list... the last item, believe it or not. I understand why my neighbor lost patience, all right.

Nice of him to intervene, though he didn't have to. Now it is done, he says, almost...

Please, stop! Have you noticed the bird? Pay attention! We don't want to hurt, not even frighten the peahen, causing her to abandon the eggs. Oh, please! Let's be careful.

What would you do in case of an earthquake? Hurricane? If a coyote attacked you? Through the hell of screaming lawnmowers you don't shift a feather. You sit perfectly impassive, an inscrutable cappuccino-colored pond.

Look, the neighbor, yelling full blast in order to top the din of the mower, has been nice. He has left a small grove around you, same shape as your body. Oval grove, oval body, on eggs.

To be honest, this copse is so scrawny that it looks pathetic. It looks like the coin you would drop into a beggar's hat. Ridiculous alms. It provides no protection and not enough shadow. But you haven't stirred in protest. I guess this will do.

There's an intersection of lines thrust into the future. I can picture them swinging, hesitant like all things that are still potential, don't quite exist yet.

At least virtually, there's an intersection of not-too-predictable timelines. I imagine them like fishing lines cast into a river, shimmering here and there, but mostly submerged. Who knows what they are doing underwater? Coming close, crossing, intertwining, perhaps getting ripped. Perhaps, drifting away.

One timeline sees the house being sold. It implies me saying farewell to this place, taking memories off the wall and sealing them in a corner of my brain. Clearly, a kind of conclusion. Farewell.

The other line involves a beginning… the eggs hatching, five chicks gaily tottering. When? Not sure. I didn't see the hen arrive. Maybe I've missed her for days, as she slyly blended with my flora. I can only approximate when the eggs will break.

Timing for the sale of the house is still more uncertain. Will the two events collude, segue, overlap? In which order? Truth is, I don't want to scientifically ponder the question. I prefer this aleatory suspension. But I can't avoid flirting with hypotheses.

Will I leave a squatting hen on the property? Will she be a bonus feature, or else a predicament, "closure will be contingent on removal of present and future birds from the premises?" Will I have time to enjoy peeping peachicks, instead, while I pack my bed, piano and fridge? Will they be my last souvenir of this home, this address, this part of my life?

Both finales sound weird. I don't wish to forsake neither brooding mothers nor babies. I would like, dear, for you and tots to depart before me, or else simultaneously. Simultaneously could be a nice ending line. Lines.

There is something ironical, paradoxical…

Since the place has grown un-domestic to me, you have found it agreeable. You would not have chosen a neat, manicured and therefore too-exposed front yard.

Still, I am presently at the worst of my land-and-house-keeping. I am keeping nothing at all. I am leaving. And you, gorgeous among all feathered things, you, my Egyptian Queen, pick this time for being my guest. As you seek sanctuary, I can barely shield you from neighbor mowers. I am a mess. My place is a mess. Don't you care?

You give me a vacuous stare. Bogus. Bogus.

Now and then I spy on you through the stained glass of my front door, which is oval and frames you just right. I have remarked that you frequently look my way. You can't hear me, not even smell me, I am sure. You know this is where your feedings come from.

You look up, neither greedy nor anxious... meek. Food might come through this door, correct, but you don't truly care. As I said, your patience is timeless. Unpunctuated. Unmarked. You are a sphinx who asks no questions.

Good. Because I have no answers. I keep filling your cup for the time being.

Your trust is my parting blessing.

~~~☼~~~

TERRA FIRMA

But what happens to the house when I leave?

Which house?

Wait. Now I am recalling an aqua-colored wall.

Now a dark ramp of stairs and a giant bag of garbage, ripped open.

It is night. We are exhausted but everything has been cleared and packed, tons of superfluous crap hastily compressed into a plastic shroud. We have to carry this load down the seven floors separating us from the courtyard, push it into the bin and then go. We are starving for dinner, craving the anonymity of the motel where soon we will sleep.

But on the top ramp we have a disagreement. About what? Of course, nothing. Tension overflowing, that's all. We stall on the steps, statues of exasperation, stubborn puppets unfit to move on their own, our strings pulled by the mighty hand of distress.

We argue. We raise our voices. Someone's hand, yours or mine, has a sudden jerk and the bag gets torn. Then it slides on its side and vomits all of its contents, now rolling and dripping downstairs with a quasi joyful chime of tin cans.

Hasty moves. That's what I recall, like hurriedly folding camp after a catastrophic defeat.

But isn't a change of residence always brisk? Sort of pulling a bandage off or sticking a needle in as nimbly as possible, matter of fooling body and mind, taking both by surprise.

Don't be duped by calm, leisurely transits. If they linger, empty a drawer today, a bookshelf tomorrow, that is a matter of logistics, not a proof of gradual, reasoned, considerate weaning. Trust me, the split has occurred on day one, with the first poster unpinned from the wall, first old toy brought to the thrift store. When divesting has started...

But *how* does a house stop belonging to us, or the other way around? Is it by ceasing to pay rent or selling the property that we rescind the tie? Sure. Though, the financial aspect is the surgical thread stitched upon the cut, once whatever viscera needed to be extracted have been. It usually takes place after we have pulled hooks, nails, screws from the walls, and we have patched the holes.

When divesting has started, home has promptly exhaled its last breath.

Although buildings don't die, thanks god. What, then? Perhaps they hibernate. As soon as we start packing, as soon as we know the romance is over, they (the premises) slip into a zombielike, quasi catatonic status. Mute and mutinous. Oh, those half-dressed walls, so pathetic...

To accelerate would be best, I believe, once we know we will have to part.

Dear house, I hadn't noticed how entwined we were, melted, insanely fusional, until we are no more. Losing you or else a lover, leaving your concrete walls or else flesh and blood is the same. Although, chances of reuniting for us are a tad slimmer.

They are slim in both instances, correct. When relationships end, partners move on. They find other partners, and so do you. Well, you are found to be exact, but you don't oppose. You surrender to the next master with wonderful meekness.

And you change, just as people do for a new relationship. But you change, for Christ's sake, to such an extreme! Your mutation is so thorough, so deep that it leaves your previous mate... it leaves *me* perplexed, dumbfounded. Ashamed? Almost. It reeks of betrayal, your sharp personality shift.

See? At the count of three you are unrecognizable, sometimes without much fuss. A light make up, a few *coups de pouce* do the trick. Even so, you tell a totally different story as if it were yours from the start. Instantaneously you bear no trace of the past, not visibly at least. Our past. Mine.

I know it isn't your fault. I have betrayed you. I am the one to blame. Also, I know it's not important. You will be fulfilled by your next match, and as happy as it gets. You always are... fulfilled and glad. You are such a good dancer, so smooth.

But how does it feel to change status? How's the crack, the in-between time when you teeter, almost naked, un-possessed? Quite divested, not yet invested again. Are you cold? Are you lost? Or do you enjoy a longed-for-break, a hiatus of neutrality, the intrinsic

31

peacefulness of being unnamed, unattached, just matter, just mineral?

Perhaps so. Such quiet emanates from empty flats, empty buildings, vacant lots, *terrains vagues*. Vague... free for once to be ambiguous and blurred, think incomplete thoughts, forget what you dreamed about.

Mutter idioms unknown. Omit explanations. Do not light up at night. Keep shutters closed in daytime. Skip spring-cleanings. Let mailboxes be drowned by unread papers. Get a tan under brazen August sunrays. Peel off. Lose a couple of gears, a morsel of fascia, piece of eave, ridiculous gable, get lighter... Skinny-dive into the next storm. Freeze in snow. Weep from every tile. Lick your wounds.

≈≈≈☼≈≈≈

SPECULUM

We called them "the vanishers." Someone tried to file the phenomenon under the "extinction" tab. But it didn't belong there. It couldn't, because of the holes. See? Those trees didn't wither, dry, perish, stop reproducing... Without a warning sign they were gone, leaving a deep gaping cavity, a scar. Rather, an open wound. They were gone roots and all, as if pulled away by reverse gravity.

Why reverse? Let's say "another" gravity, operating from a different pole of attraction, from a planet clearly stronger than ours. Wait! If such thing existed, shouldn't it work its charm upon everything? Animal, vegetal, mineral... It did not. True, the phenomenon spread following a worrisome parabola, but it affected random individuals, with no geographic criteria and regardless of species. Therefore, it was kind of inevitable to assume, to suspect...

I know it sounds crazy. But how not to believe there might, there must be a sort of agreement? At least, acquiescence. I mean, if the pull was there (that orbiting whisper, that sweet, seductive murmur, come this way, that sly siren song), some were clearly more sensitive to it. Or just willing to go.

Some... trees? Mostly conifers. Tall. Slender. Streamlined. Aerodynamic. Did morphology have an influence upon the selection? The hypothesis of "election," as I said, soon became predominant and endowed the whole thing with a disquieting halo.

Because, frankly, why would a tree choose point blank to abandon the premises? Didn't it look ominous? Like birds flying real low before a big storm, like a din of caged animals when an earthquake is coming. Like a biblical invasion of locusts... like a punishment.

The holes were bad looking, besides dangerous. So revealing, so blatantly screaming of a piece of landscape gone amiss. Like a broken front door after a burglary. Like a china vase scattered on the rug, and no one bothered to pick up the shards.

No one filled those holes either. Perhaps due to the novelty of the phenomenon, all administrations got stuck into a maze of mutual responsibilities. Private owners were also confused. Would insurance cover the costs? Were those natural disasters? Most likely.

That, of course, shouldn't have stopped anyone from throwing in some dirt and mending the scratch, thus restoring surface integrity. But it didn't happen. I have already avowed that those incidents, in spite of their frequency, made us feel nervous, hesitant, shy. Perhaps frightened? Or else... did we quietly assume that if we touched nothing the flight could be reversible? If we kept things as they were, would the fugitives consider return? That would have been awesome because the deserters, we said, were all gorgeous specimens.

Slowly, the rain filled the cavities. Lack of shadow caused rapid evaporation, and tall healthy trees have deep roots, so the job took a while. But we eventually witnessed a proliferation of quasi-identical ponds, kind of machine-made, tiny, like children pools. Trimmed with scarce vegetation. No water lilies. Ducks. Yes... they gradually settled in, one per pond, as if realizing the size suited a cellular style of existence. Private, insular. Very focused if slightly self-centered.

Those ducks belonged, of course, to a variety of species, following geographic locations. Did I say that the uprooting occurred all over the planet? Simultaneously, almost. No weather, no habitat was spared, besides the great deserts. The rain forest perhaps, just because in such mess keeping track of defections was hard.

We called them "the vanishers."

Someone wondered about possible destinations. Well, theoretically the trees might have disintegrated in space, going strictly nowhere, but that seemed improbable... Nothing hinted at a manner of vegetal suicide. Such impulse leaves a messy aftermath, a nasty exhalation that wasn't there.

On the contrary, we said the holes betrayed urgency, resolve, motivation, just like signatures penned in capital letters. Yes! The vanishers had willed themselves off, at least agreed to the exodus. If they had chosen to go, then a "somewhere" necessarily followed. They must have arrived on some rocky thing, planet or satellite.

What tickled the imagination of curious (restless? perhaps troubled) minds was how they had landed. Did the crown hit the ground? Anything might have happened as they fell out of Earth's gravity. They might have turned around, twisted, spiraled, spun... Did they ever "fall," though? As I said, we sensed their trajectory was determinate. Somehow furious. Perhaps a bit rushed? Inconsiderate? Who are we to judge? Firm.

They went, straight on, no detours, relying on momentum. Then, they must have landed on their head like upturned turtles, poor things. Did someone redress them, branches up and roots down, eager to suck nourishment from the soil, thrive again? Thrive more, as obviously they were bound (for sound if subliminal, inarticulate reasons) to find a better life.

Did someone receive them indeed? Were they expected? Foreseen? Had strange things occurred (telling signs, such as small ponds being deserted by the local fauna and spontaneously, briskly drying up)?

Speaking of duck(s), were the inhabitants of the site of destiny scared? Did they see the projectiles of wood, needles, sap about to hit the ground? Did they manage to promptly take cover? Did they wear proper headgear? Was anyone hurt?

Did they understand they were collecting, alas, stolen goods, arbitrarily inheriting someone else's riches and blessings? Or did they interpret the flood as a kind of divine punishment? Oh, no... Please! Would anyone dare approaching? Brush her finger against bark, inhale the pungency of resin mixed with whiffs of astral winds, with sweat of distance and darkness.

≈≈≈☼≈≈≈

MILAGROS

You died on a Sunday, last week. I was left with a song and a small sunflower that I stole from your garden, I admit, when your wife sent me out. Your agony had started.

I just loafed on your doorsteps, unable to leave. Then, I picked the flower. I believed I heard you say to take some of yours, and I wasn't surprised. In my heart, I begged you to take some of mine. Did you? I bet. I'll know sooner or later.

And the tune? It popped up when I started the car. I kept pushing the rewind button.

I have spent this week in a limbo, trapped between two worlds. You? I'm sure that you are also lingering, but I don't know where.

Today I tossed the flower. It was gone. I won't stick it inside a notebook. A sunflower, even small, is not meant for that. I haven't cried so far. I could write something, I guess, but it wouldn't be nice because I am angry. I know you'd understand.

Earlier on I went to the park, needing air. I sat on a bench by the pond, empty head, heart on mute, and I suddenly wanted to curse god.

Once, you told me that you loved the devil. Well, not truly. You said you had managed to forgive him, and I understood what you meant. We were similar. We always toyed with the almighty and with danger. I don't know who has won and who has lost.

I cursed god. I doubted his existence out of spite, just to piss him off. Instantaneously, three ducks flew over my head, so low that I could have touched them. Then, they landed on the lake. Oh my, they were gorgeous. See those blue rings around their neck... aren't they... the most...

I returned to my car and I took the freeway. Half a mile, then a pair of geese came across, zooming in as if on a movie screen. I thought I was dreaming. They were huge. Their belly was white. I detailed their paws and their beaks. I have no idea of where they went... a flash, and they had vanished.

But I've seen them. And the ducks. That's all I have to tell you.

≈≈≈☼≈≈≈

SUNSET WALK

Is it nameless pain, insistently loading my back, what compels me to take this evening stroll? I guess so because I can hardly move, as if lead were glued under my soles or I were fighting a gale. But the weather is nice, the air perfectly still.

Earphones stuck in my ears, I am listening to a piece of classical music, trying to espouse all its moods, passion, grief, angst, release, catharsis and rest. It's a piece by Beethoven, so it fearlessly goes up the roller coaster and down until, as a stream meets the sea, it strikes the final chord and harmony reigns. I have heard it four times but I'd go forty if needed, waiting for my scattered cells to realign and restore the whole, system, organism, I am supposed to be.

At that point my pain won't be gone. But it will be muted, on pause.

Meanwhile, I have walked a few miles, deepening into the texture of town, seeking facades, roofs, doors, windows I have not observed before. Or else flowers, trees, people. I have found them and each new discovery has hit me with a pang, a blow in the stomach, perfect mixture of marveled joy and sharp nostalgia, as it usually occurs. Each house calls to me, projecting the shadow of a life that could have been mine. And I long for every house, for every life I haven't lived, feeling both its sweet promise and its irreparable loss.

Every garden strikes me with unique botanic details, bringing back my early wonder, untarnished, at the magic of plants. And I'm awed by the beauty of each woman sitting on her front porch, resting in the lull of the evening hour. Old, poor women, casually and yet graciously dressed. The laced edge of a sleeve, the shape of a cleavage, the contrast of a leather belt against cloth, the shine of a silver ring thrill me. How a lock of hair falls, the bend of a neck, of a wrist... A small chain, swinging ankle, loose sandal revealing painted toenails... Artists didn't honor this daily display of splendor enough. Every new frame just stabs me with longing. For what, I don't know.

From a second floor, behind a curtain half-pulled, a man gestures at me. I can see that he's naked to his waist. The rest, of course, is concealed. He is asking me in, no doubt, but there's no offence in his attitude. No obscenity, if I can say. Just a tinge of despair.

I have seen this before, have I? Many times. Aren't there every night, everywhere a few loners who strip and peek out, to ease their lust however possible? Sure. I understand this urge of the flesh, this craving, so banal and yet so excruciating, so harsh.

Suddenly, I am swept by a wave of desire I haven't felt in ages. For that skin, which from where I stand seems rubbery and slick... I believe I can smell it, not yet transuding sweat or the pungency of sex, but cheap lotions and soap. I am hungering for the touch of it, for its texture that must be dense, compact, almost fake. Like a doll's.

This man of age undefined, bold and thick, reminds me of my father. I desire him and I desire that room. A cheap room, as the house, the street, the whole neighborhood suggests. Maybe half-naked, like its desolate guest.

Although I know this area of town, I have never walked on this street. I am relishing a taste of things unfamiliar and a slight sense of disorientation. The alley I just turned into dead-ends against a massive stone gate. It's the graveyard.

Well, my mood couldn't have led me elsewhere. But it's late, the gate is closed, and that's fine. A large part of me is dead already, tonight. No need for encouragement.

Which part? I can't tell, just as I can't define the nostalgia, the desire, the longing.

I start listening to Beethoven again. He died long ago, but he keeps me company. He's the liveliest thing around, at the moment. These notes, dulling my pain, are a throbbing heart within a ghost city. They are all I can hear. Plus, sometimes, the labored rant of my consciousness, stabbed, transpierced, remembering, weeping, denying. Trying to dispose of corpses, but hopelessly.

≈≈≈☼≈≈≈

DOVES

I've never seen a bird mourn.

How would I know, you ask. Isn't it something intimate, private? How would I know what birds feel?

I don't know what they feel... But I never saw a bird show detectable signs of grief, those behaviors and attitudes that both humans and animals display. Don't dogs starve themselves, don't they cry for hours when their master is gone? Cats break china or pee on rugs in hope to call back the dead. Let's not talk about monkeys...

Then it must be mammal, you say. That makes sense, as I've never seen a bird mourn, not even a mourning dove. Actually, least of all mourning doves.

One day, coming back home, I found fern leaves on my porch, up on a wooden shelf where they couldn't have climbed on their own. They were "put" there, for sure. Why? Where did they come from? No fern bush grew close-by... They must have travelled by air, perhaps a long distance, as it happens when birds build their nests.

Could they have fallen from one? I looked up to no avail. I looked down... Wait! What I had taken for leaves were triangular cuttings, neatly, nicely organized in geometrical patterns. Doubtlessly an architect must be bustling around, displaying drafts and sampling materials.

Eager to understand, I started browsing for birds' nesting supplies. Ferns, anyone? Nope. Could a squirrel… Forget it. They made dens in a select area of my backyard that they formally owned. They had never shown any interest for my scrawny front porch.

Finally I cleared the shelf, threw the cuttings away. But they reappeared, like those jasmine posies haunting Mafia's prospective victims, who find them in their purse, on their bed stand, tucked inside their restaurant menu or else stuck in their car window. "You are followed, dear. You'll be tailed wherever you'll go. This is a courtesy reminder."

I started feeling tense, but then… There it was! In the uncanniest of places, a small ledge so exposed, so at reach that I had entirely missed it, lurked a nest. Like a thief leaving clues in plain sight, the bird knew we ignore what is evident. Well, perhaps.

It was beautiful, in its own special way. Very freely and approximately wrought, it looked like the work of an abstract painter loosely combining shapes on the canvas. Colors too, brownish twigs, white fluff, bright green leaves filigreed against the turquoise of the ledge. A nest? Still in progress…

Careful not to be seen, hiding behind curtains, I took pictures of the small masterpiece. But my efforts of not frightening the builder failed, or something else intervened. The next morning, only fragments lay sadly on the floor.

I felt disappointed, then relieved. Thanks god, the bird had understood the hazards of its current address, changed its mind and set for higher standards.

No way. A brief pause and then construction resumed, in the very same spot and, of course, same style. Well, this lad had some grit. I should show respect. I judiciously abstained from documentation. Shyly, I went in and out on tiptoe.

Alas, also this second try was short-lived. Seen its flimsy nature, the nest might have tipped over. I confess that I soon forgot all about it. So it goes.

A week later my citrus trees needed harvesting and I went to fetch my picker, a milk bottle nailed onto a wooden pole. Strangely, it felt much heavier than usual. I looked inside the bottle. Surprise! A nest was stuck at the bottom, same as the previous ones, although slightly improved. Or not. The bottle kept it together, that's all.

Oh my, I didn't know what to do. Those naïve and yet stubborn trials stirred my sympathy, I admit. Should I let the bird's alacrity inspire me, leave my pitcher alone and build a new one? I lacked both patience and wisdom. Harvest was priority, I thought, and I removed the nest. Though I sheltered it in a quiet, private niche of my fence, I knew my precaution was useless. Nests can't be relocated by third parties and still be considered home.

This one vanished as well.

Mourning doves thrive around my place. I guess they feel welcome, secure. At ease, they swing on wires, peck on grass and leisurely stroll in my driveway, alone or in pairs, until I park one inch from their little feet.

They are cute. I adore them.

Mourning doves are famously sloppy builders. They don't have nesting habits besides total randomness. The task always takes them by surprise... Why? Didn't the proper skills pile up in their genes, as they usually do?

Apparently not. In the spring, each time, the couple is dumbstruck... "Now, what? Where?" They aimlessly wander until they find a box, an old shoe... If a tree comes their way they don't say no but they choose a small, shaky branch, a fork so unbalanced, so low, anyone else would dismiss it.

Most nesting attempts fail. By the time they collect bricks and mortar, so to speak, foundations are gone. As they gather roof tiles, so to speak, the first floor has melted. Someone has kicked the box or put on the shoe. They start over with equal naivety. What millennia haven't taught isn't learned in a lifetime... especially a dove's lifetime. Or even two doves.

Yes, the couple solidly shares in the effort. In the clumsiness, too. Male and female keep trying until some kind of settling is reached, often right on the ground as if they were quails, which they aren't. Fairly, they take turns brooding. They do what they can but, due to scant logistics, accidents unfortunately occur.

Doves aren't the greatest breeders. I am surprised the species has made it so far…

Not only have they survived! They are nonchalant, good-humored, see?

You don't. You say, now the "mourning" quality attributed to their call makes sense. They lament about constant loss of their estate property or, worse, of their progeny. Absolutely not. Though their tune has been described as plaintive, doves don't mourn at all. They are happy birds, which would account for their carelessness that I read as a mere excess of optimism.

"Nesting time again!" she says.

"Don't worry, my dear. We'll find something."

"Since last year the rents have doubled, I heard, and all the good deals are taken."

"Do not worry, love, by next week we'll figure it out."

And they go for another swing. For another song.

~~~✹~~~

PRECIOUS

The old janitor returned my ring with a smile. He had found it in the main hall, on the floor, he said. Not sure when or why it left my finger... When I realized it was missing I thought that it might be at school. I called. Yes. Until five. I rushed to rescue my trinket, though it was worth two dollars and had no feeling attached.

I had bought it just before Christmas, as I wandered in Thrift Stores for last moment gifts. See, in the fall my place had been repeatedly ransacked. The police had said burglars would return, and staying was too dangerous. Fine. I had tossed a bunch of clothes in a suitcase and slept on friends' couches since, not too sure about what I'd do next.

Meanwhile, I needed to see my folks for the holidays. Old, frail, sick, they certainly couldn't wait for me to solve my predicament. Therefore, though my mood wasn't truly cheerful, I had forced myself to find presents.

Jewelry was gone in the first assault by the thieves. I hadn't bought any since, not even considered doing it, until I saw the ring. It was large, flat, a disk, a pale moon, lightly and casually embraced by a silver clasp. Turquoise, almost green. Iridescent, its color constantly shifting. I wasn't sure I fancied it for myself, not quite, but I knew it was well worth two bucks... Then it stuck with me and I never took it off, besides the afternoon when I lost it.

The man pulled it out of his apron's pocket. As he handed it out to me, he smiled. And I sighed.

Suddenly another ring came to mind, which my husband had bought when our child was born. Three glass flowers, the three of us, of course. Three different colors, matching all of my clothes, and so delicate. That was also glued to my finger, so to speak, for ten years.

Right after my divorce one of the buds fell, but I found it in my purse, and I fixed it. Well, another got lost. For a while two flowers remained, then just one. At that point I guessed I should toss the spoils. Still, I certainly fought for that ring… It embodied my brief family life, my quite brittle happiness, nonetheless intense. I sure fought as much as I could.

Now this flat thing seems prone to remain. There's something solid about it. See? Unwillingly I gave it its freedom back, but it didn't run. It just waited and, kindly, the janitor… Strange that it came around when everything was gone, when the jewelry box had been swept perfectly clean.

First I thought that it was too handsome for me. But it disagrees. When I stare at the ever-changing reflections of its abalone surface, it stares back. It's a mirror. I don't ask if I'm the most beautiful of the kingdom, because I know the answer. I think I can hear it, whispered by the small stony soul. You never were, darling, but I love you anyway.

~~~☼~~~

THE DECADENCE OF GRAPEFRUIT

The tree was the first thing I saw.

I had found the house on the internet, undersized, quite a fixer-upper and not what I wished for. But I needed a home without further ado and this one was cheap. I had called the real estate agent, booked the first available showing. I had arrived, of course, ahead of time.

The tree immediately caught my eye. Gently, it soothed my nerves.

I had never seen such a tall one, though I was raised in a citrus grove. Grapefruit trees I recalled were scrawny and small. My grand folks grew oranges, lemons and tangerines in a wide, well-tended orchard. But there was no market for grapefruit, still considered an acquired taste, a bit of an oddity. The plants thrived on their own, kinky and spare.

This one doubled the house, spreading its long branches loaded with bright yellow clusters (or grapes, as the name implies) all over the roof. And it conquered me, whispering childhood rhymes, transuding nostalgia. Yes, I wanted to live in its mighty shade.

But the plan seemed doomed to failure. Complications kept multiplying. The deal painfully dragged itself from station to station, a *via crucis* without resurrection in view. When things looked really bad, I tried to pull out. Why insist? And yet, somehow I sensed that the tide would change.

I moved in at the beginning of March. That is when, from the window against which I had pushed my small piano, I noticed the face on the trunk. First I thought it was sculpted. I was told bohemians and hippies once inhabited the house... Some artistic soul must have carved it.

But those eyes, nose, lips, cheeks, were creases and bumps in the bark. They only appeared, nicely framed by the window, when I sat at the piano and looked up for inspiration. An effect of light and shadow, I'm sure, from a specific vantage... Correct.

Spring arrived, and the air filled up with scents of citrus blossoms. They inebriated me like liquor, a dynamite mix of memory and hope.

Plenty of flowers, of course, meant plenty of grapefruit. The tree was an amazing producer, but I couldn't harvest, alas. Practically none of the fruit was within my reach. In the back, I found a ladder so shaky I didn't dare climb it, and it would have been too short anyway. I looked for eco-charitable groups eager for donations and endowed with appropriate equipment. Everyone I called was overbooked...

Meanwhile, March to July, my tree spat about fifty globes a day, dropping them from so high they literally burst on the lawn. I ate some, pressed some but sure couldn't use them all and, in the piteous shape they assumed after explosion, couldn't give them to friends. While I sought ways to avoid waste I tried to keep up with the mess, as spilled juice quickly morphed into pungent, sticky glue. Passing cars smashed the orbs into mushy starfish, sadly liquefying through my fingers.

Luckily, the starfish dried up and I peeled them off, one by one, like band-aids.

But this neat disposal of corpses didn't suffice me. I wanted to salvage the bounty, for god's sake... How to get that high? Crane? Helicopter? Balloon?

At night, the fruit fell like miniature earthquakes. On the roof, on pavement, on grass, the thuds jarred my sleep. I imagined knocks at the door. An instant of panic, then a turn to the side, pillow over my head: "It is just a grapefruit," I muttered.

Tiny ones also fell. If the ripe stuff isn't harvested, babies drop. As a child, in the citrus grove, I collected them although they weren't edible. I thought they were extremely cute, and that was enough. Now, among yellow balls and brown hides, I gingerly picked small emerald pearls. They thrilled me with delight.

Pleased in my vain collection I filled a maiolica bowl, proudly propping it besides my front door. Its calm beauty agreeably distracted me from the surrounding mess until, once, a flying fruit landed in my display with the usual commotion, scattering my trophies and tilting the vase. I understood the tree's sense of humor. "I'll look for a better ladder," I sighed.

I was lying. Clearly, I wasn't up to my agricultural duties. Tossing spoils was all I could manage...

Until when a friend built me a picker of exceptional length, a tall stick topped by a milk bottle, correct... Could I have thought of it earlier? Once the fruit sat into the bottle I pulled, the bottleneck caught, and the stem detached from the branch. Now I could harvest the lowest third of the thing. Fourth. Fifth. Lowest fringes of fruit.

Enthusiastic about my new collecting capacity, I started keeping a basketful in my car, eager to share its content whenever I could. I found out that grapefruit has an equal share of lovers and haters, which is progress, of course, from the unpopularity it suffered when I was young. Who is against and who in favor is hard to guess, so I transformed my indiscriminate prodigality into prudent restraint. I decided to limit my offer to those openly showing appreciation. My front neighbor, for instance.

What a gentle woman. As she walked her puppy, she occasionally stopped and collected a fruit from the ground, lightly brushing its skin with her fingertips. I selected a few gorgeous pieces and left them at her door. Then again. She was the first one acknowledging their exceptional flavor, which of course made the waste seem crueler.

She started reciprocating my attention. Once, I found on my porch a basket of berries. Next was a carrot cake, then a slice of cream pie. I don't have a sweet tooth, but it happened to be my birthday. How could she... I gulped the thing, and I cried.

Alas, she retired, bought a better house, moved away and I truly missed her. Neighbors come and go. Trees mostly remain.

A friend learned that grapefruit rind contains a detoxicant helping to eliminate iron residue. She should grate a large quantity of peel, she thought, and daily sprinkle it on food. I invited her to self-serve. She and her husband came at odd hours, brought their ladder, climbed quietly, didn't disturb. I heard a soft rustle among branches and then found a thank you note on my doormat. Welcome, welcome.

News of my riches kept spreading by word of mouth. Two guys I had never met asked if they could make marmalade. Sure! Every rescued fruit was relief.

They harvested under a downpour, on a Saturday. Later, they sent through the mail a jar of delicious jam, labeled with a photo of their smiling faces crowned by dark green leaves I knew well. I stuck it on my fridge, with a mixture of gratitude and pride.

I had finally a list of happy takers and I had mapped a delivery tour. I divided my load in bags that I left at various doors. My errand gave me great pleasure, making me feel like Santa. The grapefruit fairy, that is.

Though my handmade device started falling apart, I tried to get as high as possible, maddened by the abundance still out of reach. Meanwhile, a food organization I had previously contacted replied. They'd come fill some cases they would bring to the homeless, downtown. Great! Alas, only a young girl arrived, with no ladder. We gathered the little we could. Later, I got a receipt in the mail, as what I had donated could be deducted from taxes. Fruit were valued two dollars apiece.

Really? Could I live on the proceeds of my crop?

It was what my grandparents had done.

The cash for my house came straight from their land, grove and trees, which were my foundation, indeed. I imagined following the ancestral ways, monetizing the overwhelming production I had chanced upon. Farmer markets. Sweet jams in fancy containers. Liquors. Curds. A complete line of delicacies. Anyone who needed an income would have thought of it. Most would have put their thoughts into action.

I had not. Why? Not sure. Didn't I own the tree? Yes, in legal terms, but I sort of felt the other way. I felt I was invested with the task of sharing its gift, which I very poorly fulfilled.

I surrounded the trunk with a ring of stones and planted a fern at its base, light green filigreed against the dark brown of the bark. I added seasonal flowers, snowbells, pink chrysanthemum. They hid in the folds between the roots, blooming randomly, impromptu, small winks of surprise. They reminded me of violets I used to find under layers of ivy, at the foot of palm trees. As a child, I was thrilled by those tiny patches of color bedecking arboreal majesty.

I was four or five. I stayed at my grand folks, where the orange grove was. I squeezed violets between the pages of missives that I sent to my mother. All that I could trace was my signature, implemented by a spread of sweet-smelling blooms. The envelope was thick, and it made a strange, crackling sound. Who knows what crumbled out when Mom unsealed it? Perhaps just purple dust, but it didn't matter as long as my gift crossed the sea, traveled up the continent and reached her in her office, at work. In the busy town where she lived, so incredibly far.

Grapefruit trees grew spontaneously, I said, in my grandparents' orchard. They self-seeded in odd corners and survived as they could. They looked funny, with their skinny branches and their gigantic globes. Orange, lemon and tangerine trees, planted in orderly rows, filled acres and acres, terracing the hillside overlooking the ocean. They were perfectly groomed, their bed neatly dug, carefully weeded, freed of broken twigs and debris. The soil, velvety and brown, was kept damp, duly and diligently irrigated. Canopies were properly trimmed, all joined in a large green roof. Leaves looked perky, alive. I followed Grandpa for hours as he inspected each trunk, snapping off cocky young sprouts with his knife-sharp fingernail. Those newbies had to be constantly pruned out, as they stole lymph from the main branches and nourishment from the fruit.

Grandpa's life was one with the orchards, organized around their needs and their miracle. Various harvests at different times of the year for different qualities of citruses could go well, badly or anything in between. It depended on smart choices, fine adjustments, alertness and infinite care. We depended upon it.

Grandpa died when I turned thirteen. Unexpectedly, but you don't usually get a notice. His last years had been shadowed by threats to the land. The town council wanted to build a mega incinerator on it, remove plants, burn truckloads of garbage instead. Grandpa fought and he momentarily won.

But as soon as he died (had the town timed it, perhaps?) the entire grove was seized. The new project implied metallurgical factories, but it was a pure scam. Huge sums were allotted and pocketed, and yet nothing was built except for an ugly rectangular foundation scarring Grandpa's gutted hill. Slowly, wild grass submerged it.

But the orchards were down in two days. Was it less? The trees were abated by tank-like contraptions, and the whole place looked just like a war zone. Thousands of dead trunks were lined up, so many they could have built a bridge. Or a railroad, spanning from my messy yard to the motherland that I have left behind.

Grandpa planted a citrus tree the day I was born, and he gave it my name. Once, he formally introduced us. I vaguely recall a green thing standing in its square of brown earth beside other green things, brothers, sisters, cousins. Grandpa planted a tree for each baby. All grandkids were honored.

I am not sure which meaning he gave to the ritual. He was trained as an engineer. He had a practical mind. But he was a fierce nature lover and a sweet, caring soul.

I haven't wondered about the fate of my arboreal twin. What does a tree matter when thousands are gone in a blink? When a pair of gutted hills is all that is left.

Once the factory scam was exposed, the inheritors sued the town council. Their claim sat on desks and collected dust as expected, for decades, until one day they won. The money was split among living relatives, a share handed to each one.

I know a bundle of bucks can't pay for a lost grove, but it paid for this fixer-upper. And for this sprawling giant... What would Grandpa think of it? Would they need introductions?

I haven't named it, yet.

~~~☼~~~

SPECTRUM

Pea-green, like the boat upon which the owl and the pussycat embarked. Or else apple-green, juicy and tart. Perhaps leaf-green, so sheer that it looks unreal... almost fake, too pure, shade of molten glass and dewdrops.

I had never cared for green or yellow before. Salad colors, I used to call them, too neutral and cool. As a child I was keen on passion. I loved pink, red and purple. Green and yellow reminded me of car trips during which I felt nauseous, and sought solace staring at the landscape with its pallet of mint, pistachio, ocher, gold. But those distinct nuances soon morphed into a muddy ribbon, mirroring my disturbing vertigo. Therefore, I started to dislike them.

Until, in my thirties, I got pregnant, and my eyes began craving a single shade I needed as medicine. Anywhere, on a T-shirt, plastic cup, notebook cover. Even a square inch of light green would nurture and balance me.

Green had been my mom's color. Not the kind now enthralling me. She wore olive and sage on her blouses, echoing her amber eyes, complementing her ash-blond hair, matching similarly unobtrusive brown, beige, rust on her skirts.

Those tones made no sense on me, a black-eyed girl with raven hair and red cheeks. I found them a bit dull but they befitted Mother, wrapping her like a second skin, a glove, a caress.

"Green is gray," she used to say. She had borrowed such statement from an old friend, a painter who had claimed it once. She just liked to repeat it. I am not sure she knew what the sentence meant. I suspect its sibylline tone made her feel important.

She did that quite a lot. She recited her favorite quotes again and again, with an air of great erudition, as if she were preaching. Those pearls of supposed wisdom were never replaced by a fresh comment, something she would have conceived on her own. Perhaps she didn't dare.

As a child, I didn't realize her lack of originality. Anyway, I believed whatever she said...

But greens are not grays. What the old artist meant is that some, those favored by Mom, function for the human eye as grays do, mediating brighter colors. For example, providing a rest after the excitement of a crimson, a canary, a cobalt.

The pea-green I craved in my thirties was something else. It vibrated otherwise. I don't know what it did to my cells, hormones, nerves or soul, what its peculiar frequency aroused. Maybe, a sense of renewal. Perhaps, hope.

Green, all kinds of it, happened to be my son's favorite. While my craving subsided, his preference lasted. I resumed my old fancies, and a sort of adult neutrality.

≈≈◊≈≈

Orange met me with the same abruptness when I approached old age. In less than a month I had sewn orange curtains, thrown an orange quilt over my bed and started wearing apricot, lobster, peach, tangerine, mango and papaya clothes. The insistence on tropical fruit isn't casual. They often came to mind when I looked at the curtains, at my earrings or jacket. I could make out their smell.

Yes, the color came with a fragrance and a kind of pleasant warmth, like a distant fire, harmless, revitalizing. I dove straight into orange as I had into green, decades earlier. It befell me, in fact, without warning.

Orange didn't bring up any memory. It was nobody's color. But I had grown up in a citrus grove, after all, spent my childhood under its trees, picking up fallen fruit, piercing the rind with my nails to release its scent. Grandpa planted a tree the day I was born, and he gave it my name. Alas, the plant is gone. The entire orchard is. It might have metaphorically returned, haunting me from inside, a presage of impending harvest.

It is not the autumn tone of rusted leaves obsessing me, though. No. It is a vibrant shade of fluttering wings, alive, tenderly explosive. It is juice spilling out, needing to be expressed, to flow.

≈≈≈☼≈≈≈

DOG DAYS

Tuesday evening you and I fought for nothing. Too tired for explanations, we slept sealed in our sulk. In the night, fires burst over the mountains as it happens each summer, alas, in our torrid region. Wednesday a thickness in the air made our breathing harder. Nothing huge, a sense of oppression, that's all. Around breakfast we apologized. Why did we even argue? What took hold of us? It all seemed unreasonable.

Wednesday the air conditioning broke in my colleague's car (the one I ride with). Two sound systems at work overheated and died. Was it due to the outrageous weather? Now I smelled smoke, though the fires were still far and, they said, under check. But the odor was pungent.

Thursday my colleague and I were sent to the near-by city of Sunland. We are dancers, and our company sells Polynesian shows throughout the month of August. It's a summer routine that we know by heart, included the address of our patrons, which are always the same. But on Thursday we got entirely lost. In our separate cars we meandered through the hills, adrift among serpentine paths all leading nowhere.

As we finally stormed in, "Luckily," we simultaneously exclaimed, "I met a mailman!" Later we realized it was the same one, twice besought by a frantic gal in a grass skirt. Did he think he had double vision? Did he take us for a kind of mirage? And why were we stranded? The air was scorching. Maybe it subtly affected our cognitive skills.

We danced in a courtyard, next to a neatly paved area where a whole pig was roasting, as required by the traditional menu. Slowly, slowly, it turned on a spit. But why was the party outside, in the early afternoon? Our audience was a congregation of sweet, smiling elders. I could see sweat beading those frail, wrinkled faces, and a lady fainted. Surprise…

One of our best acts honors Pele, fiery goddess of the Hawaiian volcanoes. We hold lava rocks in our palms and we play them like castanets. In the sun they get blistering hot but their clicking sounds, together with our twists and hand motions, are meant to appease the divinity. Well, on Thursday they didn't… The fires were so close, we thought we could hear them… a slight, persistent crackle, as if someone were trampling dead leaves.

In the evening I slipped in bed like a rag doll, a soap bubble melting with the most inaudible "pop," leaving a minuscule splash on the pillow. I was fried, to say the least. In the middle of night you got up for a drink of water. The heat was smothering, the air drier and drier, the smell acrid. As you groped your way to the kitchen, you must have bumped your toe against the sewing table. Just a quiver and yet a stack of small boxes (true, piled up in precarious balance) fell down. Beads and buttons exploded over the floor, a rain of plastic and glass, a whole carpet of stars. On my hands and knees, I gathered them all.

Friday, as soon as we started dancing, a furious customer stopped us. He had canceled the gig a week earlier, he barked. No, we wouldn't be paid. We should pack and leave. Go, go, go, he roared... The air smelled of charred animal, as another giant pig was roasting near by.

In the restrooms, where we hastily put on civilian clothes, my cell rang. Could we please sub elsewhere, said the boss. Two performers of our group had car trouble. Yes, a water pump broke.

Sure. We arrived at the new place ahead of time and we sat in a tiny square in front of the building. Tall trees promised some shade, perhaps a balsamic whiff. Earlier on, the man shouting had shaken my nerves. I wished to cool my mind, if nothing else.

Here! I had something in my purse that would calm me down. With a pair of baby scissors I began to carefully cut out paper feathers. Pretty. Light. Soft. Soothing. Then a gush of breeze, out of nowhere, lifted them in a whirlpool and blew them away... Listen. Listen. No, I didn't get mad. I laughed. I just couldn't stop.

≈≈≈☼≈≈≈

THE SALMON AND THE BEAR

Bears are right, science explains, when they eat skin, brains and eggs of the salmon and they toss the rest in the woods, constellating the ground with barely bitten, promptly discarded spoils. Such abundance is blessed, scientists say. It provides the forest and more distant habitats (where part of the residue is flushed) with the right amount of nitrogen.

Let's assume that bears know, and that's why they scatter fish all over the place. Their behavior would appear nasty otherwise. I can almost hear parents nag, "What are you doing? Think of those Biafran kids!" Or, for those unconcerned with world's hunger, "Put your trash into the can! Don't throw it on the carpet!"

Yes, the bears' behavior looks nasty, but apparently isn't. Somehow they must be aware of the environment's acute need for nitrogen, which would become despair if they didn't supply maimed salmon by the ton.

The first time I heard about it, I cringed. It was long ago and Internet didn't exist. You could not type in questions, find answers or rather a profusion of data, most of them incomplete. Yes, savory nibbles of data, and a zillion of them...

In pre-digital times, I learned the mere facts about bears' feeding habits, and in absence of justifying theories they impressed me as unexplainably rude.

Until then I had nurtured the myth of nature being wise, doing everything with a purpose. I took nature, yes, as a guide, a model to be safely trusted. In this case I wasn't too sure. Or was I? Well, I would not copy the bear.

I am thrifty. I was raised that way, country-style, saving every drop of everything. I wouldn't throw away a single piece of potato skin. A whole fish? Come on!

When I was young, salmon was a luxury. Imagine! I don't think I even tasted it until I turned eighteen. The first piece I saw on the family table was proudly provided by my brother, who had taken a waiting job in a beachside club. He had worked three solid months, the whole summer. He had returned to exact my dad's accolade, to be officially admitted into the adult-liable-responsible world.

Brother had saved like crazy during those sweaty days. Then he had purchased (a restaurant bargain) a large slice of smoked fish that left us spellbound. We kept it in the freezer, which it almost fully occupied, religiously wrapped in foil, waiting for the canonic occasion (Christmas or New Year Eve) when it will be a coveted centerpiece, its bright hue pleasantly contrasting a bed of fresh greens.

In spite of this late formal introduction, I had loved salmons since childhood because of their color. Strange, how a three-year-old could be enthralled by a shade she couldn't even define... "What color is this?" I asked the nearest adult. "Salmon pink," a smart and precise soul replied. I was hooked... I found the definition quite magical.

Yes! The fish I hadn't yet eaten gave the color a pulse, a vibrant aliveness. It added sea salt, the foam of tall waves, the smell of iodine and the thrill of summer.

Soon, I forgot the pink and just kept the salmon. What color do you like? Salmon. Salmon. I guess I had found a sort of aquatic soul mate. Traveler extraordinary, athletic, adventurous, brave, more than all willing to swim upstream. Like me, a contrary spirit.

But I also loved bears. A lot. They didn't scare me. They could be tamed, I had learned. They could dance, which I especially admired. They liked honey as I did. They played friendly roles in nursery rhymes. I could sew stuffed ones and cuddle with them, at night, which I often did.

Perhaps that is why bears' ill-mannered treating of salmons irritated me so much. I don't like when things I love do not love each other.

Lazy, lazy fellow... I imagine the bear sitting on a rock, smooth and flat, jutting out into the stream. Gingerly, its paw sweeps the water where trillions of salmons rush, desperate to go home, have sex and make babies. It is true that, once done, they'd die nonetheless... But at least they'd be done and that is what matters. See? What urges and, sadly, benumbs them is their very mission in life.

The bear breaks their momentum. With a slow, rounded motion, with the ennui of a grand lady lighting her cigarette, it curtails the salmon's élan. Hop! It grabs it, degusts its brains and throws the remnants (should we call them so? this soon?) a bit farther. A yawn and then again, as if plucking petit-fours from a silver platter. Where did my champagne go? Would you please pour me another glass? Thank you, dear.

Lazily, the bear pops fish like peanuts. The bears, to be exact. All of them, distributing around a proportional spread of corpses, alas.

Scientists say the bear demonstrates efficiency by picking the fattest, most caloric bites of its prey and trashing the rest. In other words, it saves energy. Sure. That suggests one could lick the frosting of a whole tray of cup cakes, or extract every raisin from a dozen panettoni, why not, leaving giant gruyeres behind.

If the occasion present itself, why wouldn't you fill your appetite with the easiest to get and most delicious to taste? For humans, a question arises. Who would then suit herself with the unsavory, time consuming and effort requiring leftovers? If the soil gladly sucks the surplus of nitrogen, who is going to eat the insipid and un-raisined dough?

Oh, well. There will be takers. Someone who never saw a panettone before... Someone who wouldn't know there should be raisins, chocolates, nuts, dried apricots or candied orange peel in the holes will chew the spongy thing and be grateful. Don't you know this? Of course.

There's no blame. The early bird who licked all the frosting is glad. The latecomer who found the bold cake might also feel lucky... All is relative.

I understand there's no morality involved. It's ok if bears throw an annual party when salmons rush home.

It's ok if once a year they binge, make a mess and do not clean up. A whole bunch of vegetal and lower animal cells will profit of such momentary untidiness.

Therefore nature is wise, scientists claim. Nature can be trusted.

And still. I don't like what the bear does. Give me that piece of salmon.

Yes, the one you hid behind your fork, there, under the lettuce. Close to the olive pit. I want it. It's fine. I am not picky.

What? I am not hungry, no. I had plenty to eat. I just really like salmon. Funny... I know... I can't stand a bite going to waste, and I can't forgive... It's an old thing. An odd thing. A weird quirk of mine.

Bear, I would like for you to reconsider. Please. I know you have reason on your side. Lots of reasons, indeed. I still ask you, beg you to reconsider.

Think about it. Whenever you can. In your own time, of course. At your earlier convenience, bear.

≈≈≈☼≈≈≈

BEAUTIFUL BONES

Her head motions catch my eye through the rear mirror, graceful, lively and swift like the flight of birds, the twirls of hula dancers. She sits on the passenger side of the car behind mine, and I should pay attention to the street. Instead, I keep watching her.

Although her features are blurred (my windows need cleaning), I can see that she is old. Her gray hair is pulled back, her orbits are deep and her bones jut out. Brow, thin nose, jaw, zygomas, chin... neatly outlined, oh my, aren't those bones beautiful? Still, the way her head sways as she sprightly entertains the driver is what awes me the most.

A man is at the wheel. Same age? Yes, by the candid halo of his beard. Though we are stopped at the light, he is duly watching the road. His stiff pose betrays concentration. Maybe he is lost in his mind, while her head keeps dancing.

Not just hula. I perceive different rhythms, a whole mosaic of accents, tensions, releases. Curves like questions that languorous pauses hyperbolize. Lullabying swings, hesitations punctuated by delicate nods. Extrovert, excited hops and jumps interrupting grave, solemn waves.

Why is the sight so enchanting I can't look away? Beauty in motion perhaps, or the mystery of youth eternal, undaunted, rising from core to skin. Through the mirror, it reaches me full force.

≈≈◊≈≈

A week later I notice another old woman. Once more, I am in my car, and stopped at the light. This time she is on the sidewalk. She bends over, intently focused on something. A small dog? On a leash? I can't see... Is she picking flowers? From the pavement? Come on.

Her dress strikes me, long and flowing, pristinely pressed. A nice cut, a bright color. Peach, apricot, lobster? A nuance I can't truly name, a color of flesh but decanted, distilled, intensified...

How daring of her to choose this spring shade, juicy and bold, no matter how many springs she has gone through! Not enough to make her wilt, as she apparently didn't lose her taste for things fresh.

The peach colored dress is made of light cotton. Flaring skirt, loose blouse, pretty collar. As she pulled it out of the closet, this morning, she handled it with care, her knotted fingers taking their time with buttons and zippers. But time doesn't matter. See how patiently...

What is she doing? Has she spotted a flower for good, hiding into a crack? As her hand reaches the sidewalk, the light strikes a curl of her silver hair. Her face is also luminous, serene. Maybe getting old is not all that hard. It depends on how you select your wardrobe.

≈≈◊≈≈

I remember the other one, then. The ancient memory of yet another woman emerges. Was she ancient as well? She had a scent of another era, other world.

I saw her on a small, non-touristic seashore, at dawn. I was there with my child. Near by, a man sat on his own, quiet, newspaper in hand. Four of us on a lonely beach, and no need for introductions. Nature, silence and beauty cradled us in a bubble of safe, peaceful intimacy.

The sun hadn't yet risen, but already colored the sky. The old woman was naked. She had bathed and now simply stood up, drying off in the breeze. She must be very strong if she could swim in cold water... Well-being showed on her skin.

How superb was her body in the tender glare! The flesh labored, twisted, bitten by the years, a geography of mended wounds, sewn-up scars, tiny bundles of fatigue and pain. But meticulously stitched, deftly embroidered, like a delicate tapestry.

Her nude, haloed by the rosy light, was gorgeous.

She sat, then, her hand playing with the sand, fingers tracing lines. Was she a fairy? One of the Fates? An image of destiny, as it looks when we aren't scared of watching.

≈≈≈☼≈≈≈

CREATION

I saw it perched on the fence, carefully studying the orange it held between its paws. It looked preoccupied, though not about the citrus, I am sure. Oh, no. Judging by the gravity of its frown it must be debating large matters, either the original sin (the type of fruit makes no difference, all round juicy things work, temptation-wise) or else global issues such as climate change, inequality, resource shortage... the sphere it kept turning, scanning it with its piercing eyes as if it were x-raying it, being a blatant symbol of our darling Earth. Had it found solutions? Was it seeking them? Does the impulse of fixing problems belong to the rodent genus?

I am talking of the squirrel that owns my backyard. Yes, it has a gift for analysis. Rather, contemplation. Seeing it eerily absorbed — holding delicious props it borrows from nature, so to speak, for scholarly purposes — is no surprise. But this morning the intensity of its attention was awesome, peculiar. It subliminally alarmed me, perhaps harbinger of trouble to come.

Having seen my father acting in similar ways when I was a child (he rose at the break of dawn, wrote or else meditated, pen-instead-of-orange in hand, eyes lost in a vacuum, as intent and quiet, hermetic and sealed as the rusty-colored tidbit on my fence) I knew how to behave. In spite of my curiosity (why was the beast so pensive, what worried it?) I tiptoed away.

I made coffee and sat with my cup at the kitchen table, trying to line up the day's tasks, the triviality of which suddenly jumped at me, making me slightly uncomfortable. In my embarrassment, I believe I even mimicked the inspired, mystical pose of the animal. Of the squirrel that owns and manages my back yard, correct. How accurate or else how ridiculous was my unconscious act I can't tell. Sure is that instead of getting dressed I went for another peek, to check if the lad was still there.

Yes. Now the orange, though, looked like a halved moon, and the squirrel gave me a nervous glance as if I had caught it at fault, teeth sweet with the juice of the stolen fruit. Well, not stolen, since the yard is its kingdom. All the same, alien eyes (mine) might have felt embarrassing, indiscrete as they witnessed the crude finale of its morning prayer, the devouring of the sacred object it had worshipped a few minutes before. Well, I wished to reassure it, there's no contradiction. You have performed a ritual banquet of sorts, a kind of communion. Sometimes knowledge needs to be ingested and digested. Perhaps to solve the problem one needs to gulp it at first.

Then I thought that the squirrel, at sunrise, might have simply pondered trivia, as I had while sipping my dark roast. Why not? Banal considerations, such as how to make juice... which it makes for breakfast, lunch, dinner, supper, judging by the amount of maimed oranges I find when evening comes. Maimed, yes. In spite of its philosophical poise the lad is a messy squeezer. When it bounced the fruit on its paws as if handling a crystal ball, haloed by morning mist like an anchorite on his column, it might have sought efficient, economical, even elegant ways of ex-pressing it. While it easily rules upon a whole grove (if we consider scale, the orange tree is to the squirrel a nice little orchard) my pal can be quite awkward with practical tasks. At daybreak, its mind cooled by crisp morning air, maybe it was reinventing the wheel as it comes to lemonade.

Well, I wish I could help. Teach the squirrel... See? I exactly recall my first painstaking attempts at juicing, with no press, just the help of a fork or the concerted push of my palms, hands cupped, fingers joined. Grandpa demonstrated. Here is another skill I could share... how to properly peel citrus fruit! Method one, take off top and bottom with a pointy knife, then carve vertical slits. Method two, for advanced students, the spiral. Wait! You'll get it sooner or later.

Am I wrong? I mean, is my guessing the squirrel's mind entirely bogus? Maybe this narrow vision, this three-Es-thing (efficiency, economy and elegance) is extraneous to its kind. You know what? I don't like it either. The idea of neatly squeezed juice seems restrictive, un-glorious, as I am suddenly struck by a brilliant epiphany. Now I'm sure that the squirrel, this morning, was conceiving a brand new way of slaying fruit rather than devising the best, smartest, fastest... It looked for something else, perhaps abstract, futurist. Dadaist, impressionistic or Fauve. Fauve, that is. Each new juicing experiment is an artwork, and I only happened to witness, for once, the creative brainstorm. This would also explain why the spoils are left on the ground in daring and curious, if erratic, designs. Like graffiti or mandalas, perhaps meaningful, at least from the aesthetic point of view.

Oh, my... and I clean them all with my rake, daily, in late afternoon! I clean at my best. I don't know if my job is appreciated (after all I'm wiping the blackboard to allow the next expressive spurt) or regretted (yet another Pollock's destroyed, let's start over). I have no way to verify. My impulse prompts me to straighten things the human way. All toys back in the chest. Brush your teeth. Bedtime.

I am inclined to believe that my tidying might indeed irk the squirrel. I deduce this from some active gardening it has recently done, tinted with what I'd call a shade of hostility. It has kicked out of their pots some small succulents I had planted last week... Cute round little green things, now brutally uprooted. Is it intimidation? No landscaping without consulting the boss? Does it pointedly dislike those specimens, or unplanned novelty in general?

Let's not take this too personally, I agree. Could the squirrel have tripped (after all, the pots hang from the fence where it takes its strolls or, as previously said, long meditative breaks)? Come on. The lad is a funambulist. Clumsiness in its case only applies to tedious domestic tasks, such as making breakfast and then cleaning up. Could it have deemed my decorative crops to be edible?

Healthy vegetables, meant to accompany its tangy cocktails or else freshen is mouth after a copious serving of nuts... Of course, but the greens were untouched, not even nibbled at. They had been simply ripped off. Rather, eradicated.

Which, I admit, gives me the key to such ill-mannered behavior. Voila! I am struck, overwhelmed by yet another evidence. I understand the squirrel's motives, alas. Hence, I can't be outraged. I can't dream of chasing the culprit with a shotgun, declare war, fight fauna for the sake of innocent flora...

I can't. Isn't it clear why the beast attacked my miniature cacti, tiny thorns notwithstanding? Unaware, I must have placed them on top of some nuts it buried. Meaning, in its pantry. Sitting, so to speak, on the jar where it keeps its mid-day snack, Grandma's cookies, Swiss chocolate. Had I chanced upon an empty shelf, the lad might have just swept it to make room for a new lot of provisions. All is planned, my dear. This is my world. I methodically organize it, following an ingenuous plan you impudently derange. And I don't retaliate. I only fix things (as you do when you rake the orchard, correct?) Would you please be more sensitive? Leave my storerooms alone?

Fine. I'll find another spot for the succulents, though this blind game exhausts me. Isn't there a map, a blueprint specifying where nuts go? Well, I bet it is in the squirrel's DNA, perfectly inaccessible. If I could... Unless, as for the fine art of dismantling fruit, there's no rule but a zest for constant reinvention. Perhaps squirrels hide nuts wherever they please. If the place of election is full, they remorselessly dispose of previous occupants as long as the site belongs to their registered domain.

Which, of course, opens up more troubling dilemmas. How are those domains assigned, by whom, on which basis, are they hereditary, are they conquered, are they won on a lottery, are they... But I have pondered this for too long and the quest is infinite, and I should go back to trivia, and I am late...

Wait. Yesterday night, I recall, a bit fazed by an evening drink that I really needed but perhaps overdid, after trashing a half bag of smashed oranges staining the ground like spots of red wine, like spills of tomato sauce, once again I put succulents in a vase. Over there, see the one painted sky blue, hanging within a cute macramé? Am I stubborn? I try... I try to determine who owns what, who counts more, who comes first, all that crap, all right.

As, following the train of my thoughts, I now focus my gaze onto the object of contention, as I anxiously approach, I realize the crops have been dislodged one more time. In the night or else at the break of dawn, prior to the inspired moment that so captured me. Was the trouble I sensed within the squirrel's attitude, then, related to the vandalism it had freshly performed? Silly me. Didn't I say that it feels entitled? That's its vase, where it stocks its precious nuts. But what if... I mean, could it harbor some ambiguity as cats do, for instance, when they know they shouldn't have broken, they shouldn't have peed on... they apprehend, they doubt that some kind of punishment... Could the squirrel be ambivalent? Did its excess musing, as it lingered on the fence, brow tensed with incongruous seriousness, betray a tinge of guilt?

Tell the truth, I don't care. I am just hurt to see my cacti ripped off. Miniatures, I insist. Naive, tender, defenseless in spite of their ridiculous thorns. In the vase the soil is all scrambled, upturned... Look! The lad buried an apple in the hole left by the discarded greens. I am dumbstruck. No apple tree grows in my, our, its yard. Where did it snatch this treat?

Obviously in a neighboring yard where other intruders, like me, believe they have a say about landscaping... What do I know about the extent of squirrels' domains? Well, I could research it. What for? What counts is that this very specimen is a landlord in the feudal sense. It possesses and supervises several parcels, perhaps spread on an hectare or so, inconveniently split by human-made borders... or perhaps conveniently, as those fences constitute a wonderful network, a nice web of routes allowing quick displacement and aerial, simultaneous view upon several lots. Same for retaining walls, power lines... we co-function, somehow, humans and rodents. We do, don't we?

Coexist. It's a matter of tolerance. Leave the blue vase alone, little lady. Maybe an apple tree (a miniature one) is meant to thrive there. Eden within a pot... Didn't I suspect that the squirrel might be stung with sin-related questions, at dawn, when it juggled the still intact citrus fruit? It had hidden a bitten apple in dirt a minute before! Was it trying to re-think the original myth with variations?

Stop brooding. Pick up those wounded stubs and plant them in your front yard... a drab zone, on street, the squirrel lordly ignores. Learn whatever you can about bonsai technique. Learn how to maintain a mini apple tree, if the sire of these hills and vales ordains it. Or whatever it wants.

≈≈◊≈≈

I recall my very first act of plantation... I decided to sacrifice my bright yellow bucket, the one matching my little shovel, oh well. They were beach toys, and precious at that, but August and sea season were on the wrap. Not clear yet about cycles, not quite sure summer would return, I was happy to repurpose my things, as Grandpa suggested, to allow such a fantastic game. I put sand mixed with richer soil in the bucket, pushed it down leaving room for water (it seemed wasted, but Grandpa was adamant). With my thumb I pierced a hole. In the middle, Grandpa said. Well, approximately. Deep, he said, but my thumb was short. Deep, he said, and he inserted his pinkie. It would still be my geranium, he said. Now go pick a stem from one of the thickest bushes. I came back with a branch-worth of luscious red blossoms, proud like a new bride and leaving a bloody trail of petals behind me. A stem!

Grandpa shouted. Small and without flowers. I was disappointed. I picked one and it looked discolored, sad. But I stuck it into the hole and I pressed the soil around it. And I watered... Again... Too much water will kill it! Then I left for town in order to start kindergarten. On the phone, I kept asking. How is my geranium? It's tall, Grandpa said. Fine. A beauty. Grows taller and taller.

≈≈≈☼≈≈≈

IN THE GARDEN

"Look up!" Adam said.

They were lying on the quilt she had fished out of the garbage and then thoroughly washed. She enjoyed the old, pink, soft, comfy...

"Why?"

From her supine station Eve gazed at the sky that peered through the canopies.

"See the apple?"

"Where is it?" she yawned, trying to show some interest. After all, she didn't know him that much. They had just begun dating. She should keep the conversation alive, right? Truth is, after pizza and wine she felt drowsy.

"Look how big! It seems fake."

"You are right! As if someone had stuck it in place. Like an ad for something... Do you want it?"

"No. I am full".

"Perhaps later?"

"Don't bother. Unless, would you bake a pie?"

"With one apple? That kind doesn't make good pies. The ugly ones are tastier."

"Correct... That one looks spongy."

"The skin is too bright. Must feel waxy if you bite it."

"I wouldn't. It's... an ornament."

"Like... for a Christmas Tree? Should we keep it? Memento of a picnic..."

"… in heaven." He smiled. "Baby, I think it's too high. We would need a ladder. That thing is unreachable."

"Wow! The impossible apple! Though, they are great for your health…"

"Apples? How?"

"I heard they even your mood, help you sleep, a Zen kind of thing".

"Mmmmm, do they act on your brain?"

"Yes. They are good for your mind."

"Should we reconsider? Get it, split it, right now?"

"Do you think we'd get smarter?"

"You don't need it. Me neither…"

"I wondered… I guess we're just fine. It must be the apple pie we ate as children".

"Apple pie, apple sauce, apple juice… Did you get it all?"

"I sure did! We can forsake this one…"

"Watch! Isn't it huge? Is it swelling under our eyes? Am I crazy?"

"That's the Chianti you drunk with your pepperoni…"

"No, truly! If that fell on our heads, I doubt it would make us brighter."

"Gee, you are scaring me!" But she started laughing… "Should we move before we get concussed?"

She wasn't sleepy anymore. She felt happy, exhilarated, alive. As she pretended to pack picnic remnants, she started tickling him. He tickled her back, pulled her down, and voila.

Then she felt that she knew him better, and that was nice indeed. Very nice. Hurray for the apple!

They rested. They made love again.

Angels peeked from behind a cloud because of sheer boredom.

"What are they doing?" they asked.

"Are things going as supposed? What's the wench up to? Is she done with temptation? Did she bite? Did he?"

But they couldn't possibly tell. The old blanket was thick, wise, discreet, and it wrapped it all.

≈≈≈☼≈≈≈

LUNACY

According to the moon-wheel (a bizarre little chart, correlating birth dates with the lunar cycle) she was born on day twenty-seventh. Kind of a late arrival! She barely made it! Almost fell off the wheel, did she, grabbing it just before plunging... where?

Wait. Where did she arrive from? Do we come into life and onto Earth from the universe, a wide, infinite space outside, beyond... Where would she have been dumped, hadn't she reached that slippery spoke and entered, hoopla, the terrestrial calendar? When we say "into this world," which other world do we imply?

Those were questions her child asked during their drives, home to school to her job where he tagged along, back home, groceries in between. Tirelessly, her child kept asking this kind of things. Was she annoyed? Not at all. Short of answers? Of course, but she didn't mind contemplating hypotheses, trying to explore alternatives.

Still, her son's uncanny curiosity puzzled her. Perhaps it might help to learn on which lunar day he was born, based on those bizarre games of planets and satellites.

By the way, do you ever address the moon as a satellite? Seldom, though we are taught about its ancillary quality since elementary school. We are actually hammered with the concept, to make sure we understand who is who among the stars, as if such distinction were pivotal. The sun shines of its proper light, they tell us, meaning it does its job, adult-like. The moon, poor thing, doesn't. Deceptively, it surmises a bit of sunlight and bounces it back, making believe it's homespun...

And yet such sly behavior is not openly condemned. We understand, young as we are, it does little harm. The moon doesn't damage the sun while sneaking some of its radiance. The sun isn't diminished by such minor though repetitive theft. In addition, the moon is smart enough for rising at night when the sun is absent, busy at work in the opposite hemisphere. The scam, so to speak, is not advertised. Hence, no conflict ensues.

Still the moon belongs, we are explained, to a lower category among those asters up there. Something is tainted about it, fake. Rather, borrowed. The moon, so to speak, didn't have the clothes for the ball and wore those of an elder sister. Wealthier cousin? The gown doesn't truly fit but we can't tell, can we? Because it plays so natural, so nonchalant... because it's an old salt, that satellite of ours. It sure knows its tricks.

Not a star. Not a planet either! Rather than around the sun (since it robs it on a regular basis, we said, keeping out of sight is advisable) the moon orbits around the Earth. Belated kindergartener, it signed up for the simplest task, a shortened tour. Unfit for long laps through wide, overwhelming blue, it jumped into the kid's swimming pool, so to speak...

The moon steals, cheats and takes it easy, all the things we are taught not to do. Must be why we find it adorable.

Back on track. She discovered on which lunar day her child was delivered. Twenty-eighth, the chart stated. Hurray! The two of them were close as she felt they should, she wished they would be. Only, did he come *after* or *before* her? Oh my, that was hard to tell.

Let's consider for instance those who live on the other side of the planet, meridian-wise. Those who live east of us, twelve hours away. Well, tonight is tomorrow morning for them. Are they preceding us? Sure! They have opened their Christmas gifts, while ours are still intact. They are already in the future but, wait, younger or older? As a matter of fact, twelve hours older. In the future... but older... the thought gives her migraine. Let's leave it at that.

To the point. Was her son (metaphorically, on the fictive, arbitrary moon chart) older or younger than she was, being born twenty-eight versus twenty-seven? She should answer by guts. No doubt, he was older. She knew it since when she first saw him, as they dumped him transversally upon her chest, all wiped up, she still kind-of-gooey. While she slowly recovered her breath, she suddenly met his gaze, shuddering at his wide-open eyes.

Sure, he was supposed to see nothing. But that's hard to believe in front of newborn orbs, clear, pristinely blue. Soon to fade, the nurse said, a non-color, short-lived. All babes have blue eyes for a while. Surprise… They are blind, cannot really see, can't focus, the nurse patiently explained. It takes time for them to become acquainted with the surrounding world. You bet. Then, maturing, their irises change. They acquire steady, individual tonalities. Oh, well.

Her son stared at her with his blind blue eyes that couldn't see her, all right. But she saw something in his gaze, far from empty, for sure.

Born on day twenty-eight, he was born old. And wise, like a shaman or an ancient warrior, one of those tattooed not with ink but with scars. Because old didn't always imply what it presently does, in this world, this universe. Long ago, growing old was a feat. You were praised if you did. You became precious, a treasure. She believed her child shared that kind of old… would he keep it?

Though, he was also perfectly young. He picked tantrums, got annoying as expected, loved to play, ran with friends, watched cartoons and all. But there were those questions, abrupt, coming out of nowhere, pronounced with such calmness. So direct and so complex at the same time.

It all started before he could talk. He had just turned one, still experimenting with "mom" and "dad" though his first word, as it often happens, was a more trivial one. She's not sure. Soup? Shoe? Most probably shoe... That was it for vocabulary.

He had just turned one. They were in the bathroom. She was coming out of the shower, about to wrap herself in a towel, grab him, give him a wash. Nudity had not been an issue so far, of course, but then something happened. His eyes, stuck on her pubis as if seeing it for the first time, filled up with anxiety as he pointed his small finger and stood rigid, petrified. Slowly, it landed on her. "Geez," she thought, "so darn early. I'm not ready." No doubt she had to justify her anatomy, perhaps simply but urgently. The boy needed reassurance. Oh no, she missed nothing! She hadn't been hurt or wounded. People came in different formats but all were fine, promise. Would that make sense?

As she tried to sound both gentle and firm, most of all convincing, his small face quietly sipped the words she delivered. Then his features lit up, as if he had fully understood. One-year old? No way. He must have recalled. Recognized, she thought.

In the car, as soon as he acquired language... Did he? Didn't he just retrieve it and give it a brush? As soon as his verbal skills allowed articulation, the questions began. About death. Where do we go? Where were we before we were born? Why did we?

Where did he catch such a mature thread of thoughts? Then, was it? Actually, grown-ups have no time for philosophy, theology, teleology... In fact, those thoughts sounded quite right in his tiny mouth. Pure, linear, direct, nothing tarnishing them, nothing between the source and the outlet.

She replied at her best. Well, they talked and together came to conclusions. Rather approximations, still good enough. He had points and pretty smart ones. She couldn't help fancying that he tapped into previous knowledge, only vaguely blurred. He just needed to check the viability in this world, in the now, of what his brains recalled. Verify if those notions matched adult common sense…

They talked about god. Is it male, female? How many? How important, or perhaps not? What should we call him? Her? How do they look like?

Once, when he was about five, she had to travel and leave him at home. They had never parted before. A big step. Afraid of the impact of separation, eager to insure continuity, she asked what he wished for her to bring back. He remained quiet for a couple of minutes. "Mom, bring me the face of god."

Sure, she said. What could she possibly bring? A pious image of sorts wouldn't work. It had been clarified between them that god had no given name or identity. A friend suggested a mirror. The boy would see divinity in himself, he said. She agreed, but... She thought of a stone instead. She would find a very special one, on the sand.

She did not but on the last night, as she waited for the airport shuttle, something she had spied through a shop window flashed across her mind. She could not miss the plane, of course, but she started running, hoping to find the shop open and then hail a cab. Hoping luck would bless her irrational impulse.

She should purchase the thing. Why hadn't she already? A thin silvery mask, with finely carved eyes (an ex-voto celebrating the gift of restored sight) unobtrusively hung in the midst of brash, glossy artifacts. Dull and weathered... was it why she hadn't promptly reacted? Those eyes didn't shine like the rest. Perhaps otherwise, in a slow, delayed manner. In a borrowed fashion, that is.

"I need that," she exhaled as she stepped in. She must have looked a mad woman. The shop owner, unrushed, fetched the mask from the wall and laid it upon his palm, bending down to decipher a tiny, yellowed tag. The price was a bit high. She hesitated, wanting to ask for a rebate and not daring. She pulled out the bills, making sure enough was left for the cab. She could not miss the plane. She longed, she ached to return.

As he peeled the price tag the man stopped, a bemused gaze on his face. Something fell on the counter with a light, ringing sound. Oh my, another mask! "They were stuck together," he exclaimed, and then, "you can have two for the price of one." Four, he meant, two pairs of eyes. God's face, without fails.

In the following years she and her child had other exchanges, always finding her unprepared. About tough, meaty matters... class, gender, race. She was pleased with the similarity of their views. Relieved, finding out she had little to add, even less to explain. But how could he have acquired, not yet ten, such depth, such open-mindedness?

That seemed utterly impossible. She believed he must be unspooling an inborn wisdom of sorts. She thought she could hear traces of it, in the cadence, the sound of his voice fascinating her while she drove. They invariably had those talks in the car. Was it motion activating the flow? The act of journeying? The in-between-ness? The road?

Well, it didn't matter. Would this taper down sooner or later, and then stop? It would. Her son was born old, but the wheel by definition keeps turning.

Yes. She knew that the lunar kabbalah was a cute kind of scam. Besides arbitrarily computing your moon-day, it said nothing, and for sure didn't mention future developments. As the wheel kept revolving, of course, what happened to those born, let's say, on square twenty-eight? Did they go twenty-seven, six, five, gradually losing seniority, getting more naïve, impulsive, spontaneous? If yes, at what rate? Yearly, monthly, daily?

Or, more logically, did they leap from case twenty-eight to case one? That would be quite a personality change… Was her son undergoing it? Oh, no. He only experienced a fading of metaphysical worries (insights? memories?) simultaneous to the emergency of practical concerns. Projects. Goals. Ambitions. Friends. Field trips. Tournaments. Summer vacations. Soup. Shoes.

As time went, her child started to discuss age-appropriate topics, a smooth, gradual change that she watched as you'd watch seasons shift. By default her attention reverted to herself, moon-wise speaking.

What was happening to the shaky rung she had grabbed, her own twenty-seventh spoke? Such a strange spot of maimed awareness, making her unfit for regular stuff (goals, projects, ambitions) and yet not-quite-wise. Had she already regressed to case one, walking backwards? Had she leaped instead? Did she ever stop by case twenty-eight, where the old truths her baby remembered dwelled? She doubted it.

Was she stuck on case twenty-seven? With a taste of the unknown and an itch for digging, as the universe-where-some-kind-of-clarity-reigns, reflected or not, must be inches away. And she searched, but on her own she found nothing.

How she missed those car-seat epiphanies, that pre-kindergarten philosophy, startling, freshening, exhilarating and brave. When it was gone, the memory of it melted so rapidly that she wondered if she had made it up. And where was the wheel anyway? The moon chart, where was it?

≈≈≈☼≈≈≈

SEPTEMBER

Sitting by the teahouse, I look at the treetops moved by the afternoon breeze, their soft rustle in tune with a rippling sound rising from the nearby creek. As I lower my gaze, the brown of a wooden bridge arching above the stream soothes my eyes, complementing the vibrancy of green. I enjoy even the sign listing drinks, look, for a bar that doesn't open today...

I imagine it open, and I wonder if being here with a friend I would order something. Fancy cocktail with olive, toothpick and parasol? Sure.

But I like the bar to be closed. I appreciate the absence of noise, the quiet only interrupted by the breath of nature. The sign posting liquors and juices is nice because virtual, a suggestion of pleasure I can turn off if I wish.

I should walk, now. There is much to see. Lilac grove. Thick and shady camellia bushes. A pavilion on the hillside, its white walls embroidered by climbers. A trail edged by lavender mixed with young olive trees, their small fruit unripe and yet promising.

Olive trees know me well. They directly address me, their voice piercing my cells just as their roots dig the soil.

Trees don't talk, I know. Isn't it my own voice that I hear, whispered by tiny silvery leaves? Yes. Although, I gave a portion of it to the olive trees when I wandered among them, as a child, trusting my reflections and thoughts to their serene beauty.

Then I grew up and left. But the sight of these plants, miles and decades away, brings my reflections back. The trees have kept the secrets I shared. They have preserved my soul as it was, and they faithfully replay it for me. In a blink, I cross a vertiginous distance, reaching a distant past... How remote? The trees wouldn't know. Plants compute time otherwise.

But they are not the same trees, someone could object, only the same species. True. I don't believe it matters. Maybe it is the multitudinous quality... see, this habit trees have of starting from a single stem and then spread, expand, diffuse, divulgate themselves in a myriad of fingerlike threads... Perhaps, this plural attitude is what makes me assume all specimens know what each does.

And their roots, tapping into the earth... I am sure they communicate deep and wide, hemisphere to hemisphere, all connected as it is for oceans, for water. A sea of canopies, an ocean of green.

And those seeds they spit on the grounds, through which they reproduce, are miniature coffers containing... all that each tree was told. That is why I recognize these plants and, more crucial, they recognize me.

When I'll die these trees will be around, material and tangible. Dotted with promises and full with innuendos, right here. Only, I won't be able to reach them. Only I. Won't be. The trees will.

As I leave the sloped trail to enter the oak forest, I am listening to Beethoven's Choral Fantasy, headphones on. I hum the soprano line but I wish I could be the chorus, simultaneously singing all parts. Music rises as tall as the tallest branches of the mighty canopies above me. Oaks trees are less direct and talkative than their mates, the olive trees. Equally resilient and brave but, perhaps because of their size, much quieter, more private. They let the music speak.

See, every phrase of this piece, not only the sung section, says something. Quite a simple message. *Sursum corda*, be brave, never give up. Isn't it what Beethoven always intends? He did. The man is long dead.

But his notes are resounding against my bones, striking my membranes. They vibrate through my throat, echo within my ears. The composer is dead, but he's not... I know it is common sense. Still, how common is that? What outlives the body, where, why?

My ex-husband gave me a pass for this garden, allowing me this long walk soaked in sunset glory. He works here in the morning, and I am visiting the place where he works, looking for his trace. Found. I picture him in the midst of this beauty, part of it, tiny stone of a larger mosaic. I imagine this evening light embracing him, smoothing him in.

We have been divorced for decades and no, we don't love each other, though we did at some point. We must have. Why do I suddenly feel that he's still my husband?

95

Nothing can change the fact that we have met, shared a slice of our lives. We have crossed. We can't be uncrossed. As the olive trees kept my voice and Beethoven still sings, he will always... in the past, I mean... does it make sense at all? Tenses intersect in this garden.

I have walked these trails in many occasions, but never alone until now. I remember the pleasure of nature, each time, and I remember pain. Pain when I was in the company of my husband, or with him and the baby. By then I was dependent, a shadow, mortified, mute, and I didn't know. Pain was thick like the strata of dry leaves we stepped on, in the oak woods. Pain was mine but it spread, lightly tinting the steps we climbed or the bench where we rested, clouding the glassy skin of the pond we often looked at.

Still, today I'm eager to sit by the pond or visit the bird sanctuary, another of our favorite stops. Pain has been preserved in those sites, but it doesn't hurt anymore. Slowly, it has merged with the memory of more pleasant walks I took later, with friends, after divorce.

And yet more recent memories have also gloomy undertones. As I attempted to rise from the mud of too many failures, I was brittle and broken. I was fragments, the random scatter of self that had graciously managed to survive. I was maimed, sewn back, full of scars.

My child blamed me, resented me, disliked me. I was a non-lover, non-loved, botched wife and bad mother. I can catch glimpses of those selves around. I was here with those selves. We sat by the teahouse... did we see the cocktail list? I do not recall. Perhaps we couldn't process it. We had no room yet for cheerful fantasies, not even as a joke, like tonight's.

I have been here with a friend who has recently passed. On our last visit we sat among inward-spiraling boxwood hedges, shielded within a miniature labyrinth where our children played hide-and-seek. My friend taught me the word "maze," and I was ecstatic. Raised abroad, below the olive trees, I still didn't know this term. A new language comes slowly, through many voices and a word at a time. Each word takes its place in the larger mosaic. Each word is a small stone.

Now my friend has passed. No more sitting side by side. Or, yes, in a maze with neither entry nor exit, in a place where all is kept, all is perfect like the moment when we rested, talked, and she gave me a two-syllable gift. That, you see, I still recall. That moment, that word.

I have no pain tonight, not even melancholy. I was never so clean and so clear in this garden. Beauty pierces me and it is bare, uncut. Suddenly, it makes me cry and yet not with sadness. My tears do not last.

Now I know that I'll also die, like my darling friend, soon. Which means nothing. Death, like trees, clocks around in ways we don't fully grasp. I always knew about my mortality, of course, and its impending quality unrelated to dates. But today, somehow, soon becomes sooner.

Today there is no doubt. The garden dispelled it. This place where my husband invited me, today, is the labyrinth. Here's the map, though. Someone left it on a bench. Here's the map and I see the exit, right there, softly lit and yet perfectly discernible.

I think pain or those wounds of mine had clouded my eyes. For a while I was too weepy to see, and my internal sobs deafened me. Tonight I heard words so pristine, so sharp, I understood they were ultimate. Perhaps Beethoven whispered them, or his ghost. Perhaps the trees did. Death, they said, is the golden key.

I will die, now I am sure. It has been pronounced and the verdict, look, sets me free. I will die. I will become this garden.

≈≈≈☼≈≈≈

NOVEMBER

The day after the election she kneels in her backyard. With gardener gloves on her hands, she starts cutting a chunk of wood she needs for a school project. The hatchet is a piece of Japanese hardware, by far the sharpest blade she possesses.

Still, the wood is too hard, or maybe she is weaker than usual. Though she hammers at the log with all of her strength, the entire weight of her body loading her gesture, the indent she obtains deepens at an imperceptible rate.

Impassively, she keeps at her task. More than half an hour goes by. Sweat rolls down her cheeks. While exhausted, she gets some satisfaction out of her disproportionate effort. Some of the tension caused by the election dissolves due to her strenuous exercise, and meanwhile the sun sets. Then, a loud voice startles her.

"What are you trying to do?"

Her neighbor's head peers above the dividing fence. He is smiling. She mumbles some explanations, mixed with justifications for the protracted noise. She isn't preoccupied... it is daytime and the neighbor is often noisy in his turn. Still she apologizes, humoring her poor lumberjack skills.

"I thought of a very stubborn woodpecker," he says in a jocular mood. "You should use a chainsaw," he glosses. He likes giving her tips. She doesn't dislike receiving them.

Sure, they get along, though maintaining amiability during the campaign has been taxing. As he slowly turned towards the most conservative candidate, his remarks have grown frequent and nasty. Racist rants. Tirades against immigrants like her. Since a woman countered the candidate of his choice, he has refurbished his inventory of misogynist commonplaces. Never in her face, but through the open windows she has absorbed his fervorous preaching to family and friends, reaching notes of exasperation as the voting neared.

But, yes, they get along.

Now he must be in a good mood, since his candidate won with his whole agenda of bigotry, xenophobia, weapons liberally allowed in civilian hands. He has voted for these things, her neighbor, has he? She knows his life well. She can understand why.

"It's the hatchet," she says. "It is razor sharp, but too small. This log will take forever and I've more to cut. Do you have an ax, by any chance?"

"I think so."

"Beware! If I wear myself out you will get my visit. I will ask you to help. All right?"

His smile wavers. "Oh my," he says. "Sure."

She will go. Tomorrow, she will. She needs those cuts done.

Later, in bed, she pictures herself stepping into his backyard, log in hand. Of course, she will not dress up for the occasion. In her flimsy house frock she will wander in. He will lock the front gate behind her. It will be the two of them, out of sight, enclosed by the tall fence.

She will kneel on concrete, holding the log at both ends. Stabilizing it. She will stare at the log, making sure he will hit exactly the mark she has traced. Head bent, all the weight of her body will help steadying her grip.

Her hair (she hasn't thought of tying it, too late now) will fall over, leaving her neck exposed. He will stand right above her and hold the giant ax, fit to sever the log in one single blow. He has zealously sharpened the blade before her arrival. He will hold the ax high with arms tense, extended. He will put the entire weight of his body behind it.

She will keep her eyes riveted to the pencil mark she has neatly traced on wood.

She knows he won't miss it.

≈≈≈☼≈≈≈

PEACOCKS

I'll never get used to free-roaming peacocks. On the sidewalk, like pigeons, like stray cats! How can such incredible creatures (second only to what, phoenix, unicorn?) parade among us, banal people?

For a start, they are not people. They don't form a crowd. Even when they cross path, they keep a slight distance. Like rich folks in full garb strolling the boulevards, they play indifferent, as if deeply absorbed in personal cares. Do they exchange an imperceptible nod? I am not sure. They are discreet to the point of secretiveness. Enigmatic, that is.

But no, they aren't snob! This is not what I mean. On the contrary, there is a naivety about them, mystified by their regal poise. They have the slowness of dinosaurs and the same stupor, as if just awoken from hibernation, from some sort of amnesia. And in fact they wander, aghast, in a world they don't seem to entirely recognize.

These particular peacocks escaped from an arboretum and then multiplied in the neighborhood, soon becoming a kind of local feature. Their call fills the night in all seasons, a long, lingering bawl, quite hard to define. It is acrid, disgraceful, plaintiff but with a note of questioning, as if endlessly reiterating a hopeless request, pleading for a lost cause. A wildcat's scream... not birdlike, not even aerial. Somehow feral. Childish, perhaps. Somehow stolid, obtuse. Still close to the soul, mine at least.

They start screaming at sunset. In the meantime they stroll, loaf on sidewalks, pecker flowerbeds, rest on lawns, perch on walls, land on roofs with such heavy thuds, as if not birds but spaceships, flying carpets, meteorites had alighted. On the roof they howl with increased fervor, while eagerly surveying the horizon. Looking for? A dot in the distance, a balloon becoming smaller and smaller, a very pale star? Eerie sentinels, they scan skies that for us remain mute, neutral, undecipherable, as if they knew, recalled... What?

As I said, they don't make a crowd. That is why to see many is quite thrilling. They might look alike but believe me, each of them is unique. Not a matter of color or shape, not even of expression... they have none. It's their poise that doesn't admit repetition. It just happens once. Then again, it happens once.

Female peacocks are pretty as a background, a teaser, raising our appetite for the male. The male is a miracle. He carries around his redundant beauty with sublime resignation, showing neither pride nor arrogance. Not a drop. He is innocent like a rose blooming, a tree spreading its shade, a lofty mountain or river. Still, we detect a halo of gravity, of unconscious embarrassment, as for bearing the weight of long-lived nobility or a ponderous coat of arms.

Why is he so outrageously handsome? That's a useless feature. Who could claim that if he looked like a turkey (no aqua tones, no swan's neck, precious crest, stellar, kilometric, arabesque, laced, filigreed, fantabular tail) he wouldn't be able to mate? Wouldn't females

103

notice him? Would the species go extinct? Come on. On the contrary, it's a prodigy that such monster of esthetic delirium survived. As I said, he is a dinosaur, residue of bygone ages. That is why he hops on rooftops and howls at the setting sun, at the moon… at long-vanished stars he still can see but we don't. His realm, clearly, is not of this world.

Is it by chance that this flock of former runaways (now prosperous settlers) dwell in a residential suburb, matching its manicured landscape to a T? They enhance emerald lawns, lavishly tended gardens, superb mansions lain on the grounds as casually and incongruously as the godly birds roam.

No chicken would be allowed around here, but peacocks can stride. Is it accidental? I suddenly suspect that, a banal folk, I might be the intruder within this charming hood punctuated by weird angels. Suddenly, I don't know who belongs where… who really is the stranger.

≈≈≈☼≈≈≈

ENGRAVED

Today the elephant print fell from the mantelpiece. I'm just letting you know.

Not my fault. A small rug I had placed under the frame was caught by a visitor's ring, bracelet, strap… Whatever that was yanked the fringe. The rug followed. The print ruined on the floor.

Well, my fault. I should have considered how brittle are things, how uncertain, precarious their balance. Should have known the rug was a hazard, and not taken the risk.

The glass broke and I removed each fragment, each crumb, and disposed of it very carefully. I have learned, yes, how fragile are people and how easily they get hurt, wounded, broken, ripped open.

As I hovered above the trashcan, frame in hand, shaking off residual debris, I briskly recalled when you rung me and I picked up, though I was driving. I am anxious that way. I must have sensed it was urgent. I almost lost control of the car when you shouted, "I am dying…" I remember how clumsily I swerved into a parking lot, steering with my left hand, cell phone in my right. "I have leukemia," you said " and it is going fast." Damn if I can recall what I said. I guess nothing.

I have kept many of the gadgets you gave me, thrift store treasures you unwrapped, each time, with bright, sparkling eyes. You were thrilled by the hunt, the bargain, the booty. Also, sure I would appreciate every part of your gift, the intention, the attention, the love, plus the object itself, always chosen with some special meaning. I adored the print with the elephants, dear. It was on the mantelpiece, see? Yet more prominent, since I got rid of most things superfluous. Yours weren't.

Let me tell you that only the glass broke. The artwork's unscathed. I have used the occasion for thoroughly dusting it off.

I can't grant you that I will replace the glass. Perhaps, later. I know I should. It would be time to admit it. Things are almost as fragile as people are.

I said almost. We can better shield them, with a minimal effort. At least they don't get sick. They get old, they deteriorate but it's usually a slow, gradual process and we can replace parts, renew, reconstruct. To fix things, comparatively speaking, is easy. Right. I'll buy another piece of glass.

Although… today I enjoyed the sight of naked ink, the strange purity of colors seen without interference. Glass isn't entirely sheer. I touched each of the elephants as they caroled around, so more vivid than usual. Red row, purple row. Alive, almost.

There are days when I can't look at death in the face. Today was one of those and I didn't know. I did not realize it until I hovered above the trashcan, pouring in shards of glass, making sure none of them escaped.

From the driveway, where I keep the bins, I watched the houses on the other side of the street, the trees, the pale sky of a gloomy and damp summer morning. Perhaps the absence of sunlight did the trick. I was suddenly oppressed by the distance. Yours and, sympathetically, that of all who have departed, like you.

How you slip further and further away, ineluctably pushed by something as futile, anodyne and empty as… time? What is it? Thin air, I guess, a nonentity, like this greyish and neutered sky. Yet how violent is this fall back of yours, how vertiginous. You look, feel, look… you *are* smaller and smaller. And I accuse the surrounding landscape of hiding you, blocking your way with its sealed, opaque surface. I accuse it of treason as if it, the landscape, slyly concealed a crack, a pinhole that would allow me to reach you, you to reach me or at least get within ear's range and shout…

Hello?

Incidentally, here is a detail I'm sure you would appreciate and I was forgetting. As I caressed the elephants, brushing their silhouettes (although aware I shouldn't put my fingertips upon artwork, I couldn't resist…)

As I outlined the noble, grand beasts you once confided to my care, I realized an ant had crept among them. A real ant, now a corpse, printed on paper as well. Etched, its tint shifted over time into an eerie color of rust. Perfect pattern, precious, minute design. And ridiculous, if juxtaposed to the cohort of pachyderms it had dared approaching, as if it had wished to acquaint them, to join the lot.

I swept the corpse away. It dissolved, like ashes, into a pinch of invisible dust.

≈≈≈☼≈≈≈

FIVE SENSES

They are walking up the graveled road leading from the gate to the house, a straight, dusty lane where they like to linger. Now and then, Grandpa stops to detach dead flowers and leaves from the geranium shrubs bordering the path. The plants are overgrown, juxtaposing in chaos and profusion.

She adores geraniums. Each bush blooms in a slightly different color. The entire red spectrum is there, and you wouldn't believe how many variations exist. The Inuit have eleven definitions for snow. She has more for red.

When such a great pallet strips under her sight, her eyes pick a favorite. Her eyes usually put the things they like in a sequence, going from pretty to marvelous. What a blast is moving from Caramel Peach to Queen Cherry through Rose Ballerina, Pink Fairy, Crimson Fire and Strawberry Moon! It is shifting from happiness, to bliss, to the maximum currently available ecstasy. A lot, but she can manage it. She hasn't overdosed yet.

The other senses don't act like her sense of sight. She is not compelled to choose favorite songs, food, smells, or wool sweaters. Those things are more equal.

About songs? She doesn't prioritize among those Grandfather belts out when he is stuck in traffic. First, his fingers drum on the wheel as if he were mad. Then his booming voice detonates. Half a stanza, a fragment of chorus, whatever he picks makes her happy.

Does he sing in tune? Hard to tell. She should know the tune and she doesn't. Is he a tenor, bass, baritone? Her musical jargon is poor. Not a lot of subtleties... She only has achieved those for color. Years later, when she'd know the difference, there will be no way to play back. Her ears won't remember Grandpa's pitch accuracy, not even his range. She will wish her listening organs were better conceived. Larger storage areas, perhaps?

The road is squeezed between mountains and shore, cars progressing bumper to bumper. There is no other way to get home. On her side, very close, is the ocean. Waves break against rocks, slightly frightening. Slick, sinuous like a cat's backbone. Proud and unreliable. Waves make sound... an obstinate, powerful drone.

Sounds are waves. They bounce back and forth in the car while Grandpa imperviously modulates. They rise, fall, overlap. Like the ocean, music is one. You can't really take it apart. Don't have to.

Grandpa teaches in songs. He is homeschooling her, right. In songs? Yes, for several reasons. First, he must have realized how much his voice pleases her. Although he watches the road, he says, he has caught her smile out of the corner of his eye... Strange. Eyes don't have corners. She draws perfect circles with long, starred lashes.

But it's true that his voice makes her smile, sometimes laugh, and therefore Grandpa's teaching is fun, a wonderful game. Foot glued upon the brake, he sings the multiplication table while they creep like snails on a cabbage leaf. He has set the entire thing in duet form. As he intones the question, she chirps the reply. They go from one-times-one to ten-times-ten. A hundred, the top limit, looms higher than the sky. When she'll memorize up to a hundred she'll have reached eternity. How nice of Grandfather to hand down such a precious tool! She is eager to acquire it, still working on it. Ironing a few kinks and wrinkles, a blurred little spot between seven(s) and nine(s).

Grandpa's second reason for teaching in music is shape, she supposes. Sung words, phrases, periods, are rounder than spoken ones. Smooth like pebbles, they cozily niche in her brain.

Songs are secrets as well. They are riddles you don't have to clearly understand. They are whispered jokes... though you don't truly get them, they still make you merry. Grandpa croons, "Creole, with your dark aureole," or, "You will be my Starshine." Who is he talking to? No one else is listening. Who's Creole? She must be. Has been. Will become.

Both her grandparents trust her. She is four and yet on grocery days they leave her alone at the baker's, to expedite their progress. "Don't you move until we come back! No run in the street. Promise?" Sure. It's a ritual. Meaning, all the talk is pretend, like a game of sorts. She'll stay where they put her. They are not really gone. They are just out of sight. She is still one with them, attached, undivided.

When she is tired, she slightly leans against the counter, her cheek cooled by the aluminum. Is the smell of yeast inebriating her? Fermentation has such effect. Her first shot at intoxication, enthralling. She breathes in.

The ovens are hardly visible at the very back of the room, which sinks into darkness while up front all is white. The employees have candid aprons and caps, arms and faces sprinkled with flour. Chubby balls of dough are snow-capped mountains. They are lined up on huge wooden boards, like giant oars, nimbly swung around by the bakers.

Loaves land on the boards from nowhere (a fine dust blurs her sight). They alight with a plop, equidistant, a row of teeth inside the ogre's mouth. The ovens gulp and then spit them. When they exit they are golden and crusty, hard and somehow less charming. Their smell is divine.

Good girl. She hasn't budged. Grandpa gives her a roll embellished with miniature horns. The inside is both airy and fleshy. It melts on her tongue.

Our bread is like cake! Grandpa brags. They live in the baking capital of the country, and such feat makes him immensely proud. We don't need dessert! He ends the meal with a morsel of crumb, the ultimate treat, and a small bite of fruit. Bread and grapes, bread and oranges. Perfection.

She agrees. Bread can be delicious. What isn't? She still dislikes nothing. She is exploring diversity and enjoying discovery. Rice is grainy, gravelly, multiple. Pasta is smooth and slippery, playful, a good sport. Parmesan is strong, piquant, precious, to be handled with care. She is filling her own encyclopedia. Nothing wins the prize. If a box of chocolates is passed around, oh-so-rarely, when a special friend comes for tea, she takes one and savors it. She never expected second servings. They were never offered.

And yet, she has a favorite. A bun Grandpa wraps into a napkin and then solemnly sneaks inside her wicker basket. Two thick slices of bread and one of gruyere that she'll eat whenever she wants, during her lone wanderings. In nature, unlike in town, she enjoys ample freedom. Wild animals, snakes and ravines are nothing compared to cars or ill-intentioned humans. Her strolls have no limits besides dusk or hunger.

The cheese with its rubbery thickness gives strength to her legs, fills her stomach. She squats on a rock, slowly munching while she stares at the ocean, below. Once more she has made it to the very top of the hill. Here the wind is strong, but it doesn't bother her.

Yes, this is her favorite food. Taste isn't the point. Freedom is.

Ice cream, then. A cone. Lemon, please. Ice cream isn't food, but a bargaining item. Grandpa hates driving to town alone. He invariably asks for her company, and she jumps on the occasion. Sometimes, though, an urge to remain with Grandma makes her vacillate. A fear of neglecting her, a vague need for balance, an itch.

She doesn't prefer Grandma to Grandpa. About the other way around? Of course, not. No winner and losers, no grading is yet in her system (except for red shades).

Sometimes she opts for Grandma out of blurred but pungent concerns for equality. Justice.

Grandma goes nowhere on her own. She can't drive. No female of her generation does. She is given a ride if her presence is sought, if she has an errand to run. Home is her domain otherwise, a place not devoid of attractions. In midafternoon, when Grandpa leaves after his siesta, house chores wind down a bit and Grandma has some rest. She sits by the window because of her sight, faint in spite of the reading glasses she stores within embroidered sleeves.

Here's an unforgettable icon... a dark silhouette contoured by a luminous halo. During the afternoon pause (mirroring the wee hour, the stillness of three-to-four a.m.) Grandma likes to read poetry. Today, maybe, she will recite some aloud.

Now, what kind of pleasure is this? Hard to pinpoint. It is draped in black lace, like Grandma when she dresses up. It is a medallion, a cameo, one of those ornate things stored in the rosewood glass case... She often admires the collection, both intrigued and awed. Those curios are like parmesan, she sums up after lengthy pondering, to be enjoyed with parsimony. With adult permission, of course.

The same goes for poetry. It comes in small doses, interspersed with long silences. Tears linger nearby, wrapping words in a mist no matter their subject. Which isn't the point anyway.

As for songs, poetry is differently shaped than mere conversation, and it doesn't sound like fairy tales (of which her grand folks are generous). Oh no. Fables are speech, only spaced, a bit magnified while poetry is thin, oblong, thready, sometimes frayed, fringed with small crystal beads.

When Grandma entices her with lyrics, her eyes pointing at the window—a small haven, a curtained cocoon—Grandpa threatens ice cream. In town, he mellifluously says, there could be a cone. Magic spell. No child would refuse without tainting her reputation. It's a password, a code. Being promised ice cream means no choice is left. Your presence is mandatory. You have been recruited.

Grandma has a soft spot for salami, dark chocolate, coffee. She treats herself in tiny portions she religiously absorbs, focused, with a kind of frown on her face. Is it delight? Apparently, but it also feels painful. A bit scary, bit shameful... is it why those things are called "weaknesses?" Like a residue Grandma should have outgrown, like tantrums or peeing in bed, things adults don't do. Grandpa doesn't have weaknesses. Besides bread, but that's a municipal glory.

Sometimes Grandma describes her old dresses. Well, because she insistently asks. She likes to hear about things that she cannot see. Past things, utterly gone, not even concealed in those drawers either stuck or else locked-and-the-key-got-lost. No. Things disappeared, like the dead. Her eyes shut, she listens and makes her own picture. It's a complex and layered pastime.

Grandma's old clothes (where are they? god knows!) appear three-dimensional, thick, tactile even when, as it happened, they were made of "Georgette." A flimsy variety of French silk, Grandma specifies as if it meant something. Well, in spite of her ignorance she accurately guesses its qualities, its caressing feel, grace imponderable. Its affinities with love... sensuality but also fragility, inconsistency and the habit of vanishing into thin air, poof, gone with the wind. About the opalescence, see-through-but-not-quite? What does she know of love? Nothing, and yet Grandma has managed a crash course through her fashion reports.

Crepe Georgette partakes in the bitter-sweetness of chocolate, coffee and salami. It is another weakness of Grannie, but how to resist it? A cloth named like a girl can only be special. Isn't a dress made of it, necessarily, a friend? A soft doppelganger. If you wear it, you are not entirely alone.

Does loneliness underscore yearning? Like a lining of sorts? The blues tainting Grandma's pleasures suggest it. She can feel it like sand in her sandals, a rock stuck inside her shoe, a pea under her mattress. She cannot name it yet.

During their engagement Grandpa painted dresses for Grandma. She had them sewn and he decorated them with flowers, birds, feathers. Which color? Nothing near red, darling. Sky blue, periwinkle, peach, cream. Not everyday clothes, they were worn on special occasions such as concerts, opera, theater. Otherwise they were religiously kept in a closet.

Then, those garments were useless, like the silver toys and odd china locked up in the display case, sunk in twilight in spite of their pride. Still, your fiancé painting one-timers seems glamorous, the kind of exquisiteness she would want to grow up for, correct? Oh yes, to be engaged sounds promising.

Marriage? Its dullness, alas, is made obvious by the very same story. By the fact that those pretty gowns were never worn after wedding (she has worriedly inquired). Could you imagine Grandfather painting for Grandma, nowadays? Not even a kerchief. Or else promising ice cream to lure her to town? Forget it. Married status must be a drab upshot of engagement, a slight indigestion perhaps, after excess bliss. Could she just... Creole comes to mind, the brown-haired girl of the song. Who is Creole? Did she wear Georgette?

Until, once, she finds where those outfits have gone. She unburies scraps of fine cloth from the ragbag, very small but certainly precious. No painting, not a single trace. Still, the charm of chiffon is there, unmistakable although brittle, crumbling away as she touches it like some archeological finds in daylight. You look at them. They disappear.

All colors have thickened with age. The original shades are lost, and yet briskly revealed within folds, when seams come apart. The jarring contrast between pea green and olive, between peach and rust, pink and brown, enthralls her. How did that become this? Bizarre alchemy. These scraps always sport a detail betraying incompleteness and inviting repair, reconstruction. Hook, fastener, strap, buttonhole. A corner of lapel, cuff, pocket... pathetic and forlorn. She worships these precious remains, these worthless gold nuggets.

She should not play with them, Grandma says. They are dirty. They ate dust for decades, or dust ate them, just manners of speaking. She volunteers washing them. Alas, it is impossible. Water only would hasten their passing. Too bad. She adores washing, so much she has decided to make a career of it. Washerwoman. Not clear why both Grandma and Grandpa find her choice hilarious. They make no comments, just laugh.

She is readying herself for the job, making sure she masters it, though she already feels pretty confident. She's allowed some practice with kerchiefs at the kitchen sink, which is relatively low, though she needs a stool. They let her peruse the wooden board and Marseille soap (Grandpa has sliced a piece she can hold). She loves water.

Does she? Here! Let's make watercolors with children paint. A ton of old magazines shields the oak table, while Grandpa attentively watches. Oh, the sight of paint shifting on paper! Small pools sliding, twirling around. She picks complex subjects. Always people, mostly washerwomen, perhaps future ones.

She likes plasticine. Six sticks in a box. Grandpa demonstrates modeling basics. Here! He tapers balls into eggs to make heads, rolls thin cylinders for arms and legs. And then he mentions clay, the thing planters are made of. Could she have some? When? Soon? She is eager to touch it. She dreams of a pail full of silky, milk-colored slur, her hand slowly mixing it.

Clay, Grandfather says, feels like earth. During one of her wanderings she squats in a tree bed, with soil soft and pliable. She has carried a bucket of water along. Slowly, she adds fistfuls of dirt and she mixes them thoroughly. Then, she makes a bear. A few balls, large for body and head, small for paws and smaller for ears, pushing each piece as she goes against a stone wall. She pokes eyes and mouth with a stick. The bear looks alive! She admires it in silence, ecstatic, eager to share the news.

Not yet. Strange… she feels she should wait, keep the surprise for later. But a secret, alas, is kind of embarrassing. It takes too much space, squeezing everything else pretty tight. Let it go, make room, breathe! As tasty as you wish, secrets hinder you if you don't dispatch them on time. She hesitates. Should she? Should she not?

The day after, a friend comes to visit. Grandma serves tea and buttered rolls in the dining room, and before the guest leaves she calls her for meet-and-greet, briefly, as it is appropriate. Grandma's girlfriend might be too benevolent, Grandma a tad more joyful than usual. So much adult gladness detonates a chain reaction of sorts, and her secret abruptly overflows.

She can't help confessing her deed. Uncaring of town shoes, high heels, long skirts, she begs the old ladies to follow her. They should come see the bear! They oblige, giddied by her feverish enthusiasm.

She is sure of the place, but there is no bear. Grandma smiles. It has crumbled away, she explains, the sun causing moisture to evaporate. Dried soil didn't adhere to the rocks. It is normal. Or else, someone watered the plants and then hosed the wall. The statuette melted into mud. Will she make another one? Soon? Of course, they believe her! Of course she didn't lie!

That wasn't the problem. The two old women stumbling about weren't either. Unaware of their trouble, she has no regrets while they teeter back to the house. But she's fighting tears she'd better not shed at the moment. Instinct tells her sorrow, like her secret, should be kept for later. Hold on. Not sure why, and anyway it is impossible. She is horribly sad for the bear, untimely passed, and in solitude. Stillborn little cub.

≈≈◊≈≈

They are walking the graveled road leading from the gate to the house. Fall has started, but the weather is still pretty warm. She isn't schooled yet other than in songs. Hence, she isn't forced to leave. She will at some point.

Here's a birthday gift, Grandpa says. How so? Her birthday is in the very middle of winter. By then she will be gone, so he has bought her an early present. She will carry it in her suitcase, a memory of Grandpa and summer. As if it were needed. He hands a package to her, oblong, tightly wrapped in brown paper and tied with a string.

It feels like a roast. Is it meat? Guess! He says. Yet another game to fill the long stroll. Grandpa never wastes time. Here, he stops to free stubborn geraniums of their dead appendages. If he cleans them they will give more flowers, he states. As if his mere diligence could forever prolong the season...

They linger. He hops on top of the wall to reach the orange trees hovering above them. With his thick thumbnail he gets rid of unwelcome sprouts, sucking lymph the main branches need. He never wastes time.

Meanwhile, she tries guessing. She palpates the softness under the wrap, promising but mysterious. What is this? She doesn't feel smart, and a knot is squeezing her throat. Later, in the kitchen, Grandpa cuts the string with the scissors, rolls it tight and then folds the paper.

A doll. Soft, yes, kind of rubbery. A blond lady with blue, round eyes without corners, staring straight ahead. She looks like her mother, which is nice, comforting, and not. She loves her. She loves her. She will make her a brand new dress, not light pink like the one she's wearing. A straight tunic, out of scraps from the ragbag, the color of rusty autumn leaves.

Before she goes home, Grandma says, she should be initiated to the alphabet. She is four and a half. Old enough. They have time on their hands in midafternoon, when lunch is all wrapped-up and dinner still far. She should learn and then she'll read poetry, alone. She never thought that a necessity. She thought poetry an in-between pleasure, like waltzing. Like something you pour, wine or water, from pitcher to glass.

But Grandmother wanting to teach her is generous. She is willing to try. First thing is to separate vowels from consonants. As soon as she'll grasp this basic distinction they will proceed. Grandmother chants vowels in order, five, like the five senses. Like the very day she was born, her birthday, for which she has just cashed a gift. Five isn't too hard to remember. Good number, with a rise, a peak and a fall. A mountain.

While Grandma recites, she keeps her eyes closed. Who knows why she visualizes the dining room cupboard, filled with blue china bowls? Eyes shut, she tilts the bowls until their concavity faces her. With their round open mouths the bowls vocalize, naively, childishly spilling sound. Those bowls do not have secrets. They sing songs in five shades of blue.

Now vowels are safely shelved. Consonants are helpers, Grandma explains, and immediately Mother comes to mind. Help Mom. The two words are inseparable. Help Mom with home chores. Mother hates them. She is tired from work. Helping Mother is something she craves. It means being with Mother, who doesn't have time otherwise.

A long row of pressing irons appears under her eyelids. They are backlit, their shapes neatly drawn against a windowpane. Don't they look like mice? Grandma always treats them carefully. They are heavy and old, unhinging like boxes when they are fed with charcoal. They are miniature ovens. A long line of irons, each at work on a strip of linen, stark white. Dear consonants. They are quieter than vowels, more adult and responsible, wiser. They know how to keep secrets. She thinks she understands them.

Back in town with her parents, in winter, she'll start school. When spring and the swallows will come she will return South, Grandma promises. Right. She begins waiting for spring without further ado.

≈≈◇≈≈

The following summer, Mom joins them for a week or two. She is five, going to six, and once more they buy her birthday present too soon. Light lingers until late evening. They have lots of time on their hands. Mom, more modern than Grandpa, thinks the girl should be allowed to choose, so they drive into town (same old crowded road, sea on the driver side, singing Grandpa). In the toy store, a wide spread of items confuses her. She is blinded, wordless, and stuck.

Mother takes the lead, offering a simple alternative. A bead box (a kit for making jewelry), or else a doll. Pick! As if the two were comparable. The bead box is sheer multitude. True, the beads are plain wooden balls, same size and same shape, but they come in a rainbow of colors. She imagines threading a necklace. Her hands ache with yearning. They would salivate if they could.

But beads don't keep company. They are mute, and after you have done the jewelry none is left, while a doll is a friend forever. She can't choose. Mom does. Look, things don't need to happen at once. Let us leave the box for next year. Take the doll.

This is very hard, very sad. Next year might well come, but she doesn't feel she can count on it. The box makes it back to the window, to lure other passing girls. Two small dolls are brought to the counter. Why two? Who thinks abundance is best? It's redundant.

The dolls are identical, says the vendor, one in red, one in blue, that's all. He points to their dresses, shoes, bows. How could red and blue be the same? They are separate worlds, as distant as galaxies. Oh my, the sobriety of blue, reminding of Grandma, chanting vowels, ink flowing from the pen, the notebook she is filling with letters. But then the gaiety of red, geraniums and cherries, tomato sauce. Beach umbrella, ball, bucket and shovel. The sunset.

She is paralyzed. I am sorry, the girl can't decide, Mother says. That's all she remembers. She has forgotten if one doll was bought and which one. If someone was moved by her confusion, therefore interceding for both. Did the employee add a box with some plastic beads? She knows she felt ashamed. Since, she dreads the word "choose."

≈≈◊≈≈

Back home, Dad plays classical records on the gramophone. It's not Grandpa singing, but it is a pleasure of sorts. With her eyes shut (once more) she guesses composers' names. Not so difficult, though she doesn't know those are people. She believes they are kind of brands, like for cars, defining colors of sound.

Yes, music has colors. Like the human voice, right? When people are speaking she sees clear, distinct hues, very useful for keeping folks organized. She can group them, let's say, in neat chromatic zones. The garrulous yellows. Moody indigo. Plosive orange and red. She doesn't share her observations, persuaded they are obvious.

Once, following something she blurted out at dinner, Dad gives her a strange look. "You have a sixth sense," he tells her. He is usually mad at her, therefore this must be bad, an extraneous growth, a monstrosity. Like being born with an extra toe (it happens, Grandmother said). What could a sixth sense do? Nothing at all, she concludes. It must be a way of speaking, maybe a kind of curse. Poor Dad has paid her a compliment, or intended so.

≈≈◊≈≈

Decades later, the scent of geraniums comes back. On a bus, perhaps the underground of this or that town, abroad, always. It is not in her nostrils. It is in her brain and it's sharp, distinctive, but there's no flower around.

Once, she inhales it from the skin of her lover. Her first "loving" one... more casual encounters smelled usual. He does not. She tells him, but not very insistently, unsure about how he'd take it. Of course he's not wearing perfume. By the way, no perfume is made out of those plants. But a trace of that unmistakable fragrance is all over his body. As she notices it, she doesn't remember the road, the roadside, the bushes. Too much time has passed or else not enough.

Then she does. The scent must have been on Grandpa's fingers, stuck under his nails. She recalls, yes, the velvety leaves of geraniums. She smells velvet like skin, under fingers, and the lingering road, summer ending, Grandpa long dead, still blooming, still blooming.

≈≈≈☼≈≈≈

AT RISK

I don't know why I do this. It's a lost cause and a loss of time, of which I have little. Wasting it overwhelms me with guilt, but I avow that I don't feel guilty at the moment. A bit torn... Part of me (ego, rational mind?) tries to stop me, pointing at a more sensible course of action. Toss those flowers, which are clearly dead, logic says.

Stillborn, rather than dead. They have only arrived yesterday. They are sunflowers, my favorite kind and I hadn't... I hadn't had any flower for ages, and I didn't expect these. Hence, they thrilled me with delight. I chose a delicate pitcher, modest, pale, further enhancing their boldness, and I prepared myself for protracted enjoyment, as they can last two weeks with a little chance.

But this morning the heads have already dropped. I guess the bouquet was frozen previous to sale, and the crowns won't open. They will simply wither and fall. I have duly shortened the stems, cutting them at an angle. Now I am doing it again, just in case. I have put nutrients into the water, to no avail. These sweethearts aren't wilting because of my carelessness. Not my fault, no! The bunch is a scam... Well, the bunch has done nothing. The florists have.

Why am I making these complex wire structures? Dark green, matching the stems... Though I ingenuously coil them and bend them they cannot support the crowns. No, they simply don't work. I insist, trying different tricks until each head is propped, more or less, in standing position. How pathetic! I know it will be useless. I am consciously setting up a sad masquerade. For my own sake? I guess. These sunflowers, if not already gone, are in agony, but I have to pretend that I'm rescuing them. At all costs. I am doing the impossible, yes. Poor flowers, poor flowers.

One more day and they are corpses. Kaput. Nothing now can spare them a trip to the trashcan. Should I do it at once, without hesitation, then forget all about it? Oh, no. First, I have to remove the scaffoldings I have meticulously attached to the stems. I can't toss these either. Poor wire. With a pair of pliers, the same I've used before, I painstakingly undo every coil, neatly rolling it onto a spool. I take crutches off my dead babes as if pulling nails from a crucifix. But I am the one bleeding, I swear.

I wish I were so kind, so compassionate to my fellow human beings. I wish I were so tender, so irredeemably in love, with myself.

≈≈≈☼≈≈≈

THE STATUE

The statue was life size, perfectly realistic. A man in business suit, attaché case in hand, faced a building, standing a foot away from its wall. His neck sharply thrust forward, his head partially buried into concrete, he appeared to have intentionally struck the façade, oh yes, with the very top of his skull... In a rage? In despair? The effect the artist sought wasn't drama, I am sure, but eerie surprise. Mostly achieved.

On my way to a weekly commitment, I always gave the statue a glance. Over time, it had become a landmark. It was placed up a ramp of stairs, in the forecourt of a lonely skyscraper, distanced from the area where people strolled... well, not many, as the neighborhood was sparsely lived in. Perhaps, then, the poor guy was pouting, disappointed by his lack of exposure, saddened by sheer neglect.

I walked by just after sunrise, while night dampness evaporated in fog and all colors, still, were a muted pallet of grays. At that hour most of us bury their head in the pillow, pulling their blankets up for an extra measure of sleep. The man's gesture didn't feel utterly absurd, notwithstanding the hardness of the material he had chosen to hide from dawning reality.

Only a bit of excessive strain, an exaggerated tone of fatality bothered me. Yes, a feeling of "how do I get out of here, should I change my mind," hit me sideways, slightly making me cringe... But I didn't linger on it. After all, the thing was a sculpture, correct?

I had never seen folks getting close, not even watching that fellow. He was distant from the main sidewalk, I said, and at daybreak any business the skyscraper might host would have been still dormant. No one went up the steps leading to the forecourt, and no one looked that way. Only a tourist (they are early people) sometimes stopped, took a snapshot... Otherwise the statue kept strictly to itself, isolated, ignored.

Except, once, three people stood near it. A lone man, and a woman with a little boy. They were slightly in retreat, upstage, I could say, their back to the wall of the building. Common sense suggested the presence of something behind them, maybe a double door or a lift. Maybe an office of sorts, where that morning supposedly something would happen. Had a bank, located at a higher story, added a money machine at ground level? From the sidewalk I couldn't quite tell. Maybe a line was forming...

Not truly. The trio in wait was split on either side of the bronze, at which they seemed to look. They kept still, in the limits of human capacities. That seemed natural for the single man, more surprising for the mother and son, aunt and nephew, whatever. And the two communicated, indeed, but occasionally and with scarcity of means. Here a nod, there a frown or half of a smile... now and then the grown up checked on the child's patience. Hold on, love. Hang in there.

But what were they doing? Sorry... how would I know? I walked by, which isn't a fair opportunity for deep, thorough analysis. Just for fleeting impressions. And hypotheses, very likely wrong.

But impressed I was. If the statue was meant to be eerie, its effect was nothing compared to the absurdity of that living tableau, as from my point of view (incomplete, I admit) the three seemed to wait for their turn to take the bronze's place.

Had they arrived that early to avoid the long line, hoping to beat the rush? Even at a distance, I could see the trace of sleep interrupted and a slight anxiety... that tension, when you expect for your number to be called. And I couldn't help picturing a mob swelling, pushing, tickets in hand.

What for? What did the statue advertise?

Maybe a brand new form of massage. Yes, a special device would hold your brain from all sides, with no allowance, not even a sixteen of an inch. Everything in your mind, so compressed, would fall into place. No room would be left for hesitations or doubts (those disturbing loose ends). Alien thoughts, extraneous juices would be painlessly squeezed out. A great thing to get on a Monday morning, for instance, before work. Or the other way around, on Friday afternoon...

Wait. That didn't sound right. Something in the angle of the man's neck denied relaxation. A deliberate effort, a strong, clear intention were evident. Was there something worth seeing on the other side of the wall? Or rather inside, like a peep show.

Porn? Certainly not. Wrong location, wrong hour, wrong crowd... although you never know. Fabulous vacation landscapes, to relieve urban claustrophobia? I doubted it. Too banal.

It had to be something more personal, urgent. Here we go... You'd see your dead ones, as if they were alive. Yes. As long as you had sent in pictures on time your dead would be there as holograms, shockingly tridimensional, and you could talk with them, ask whatever you wished. Perhaps they would respond, or at least...

You could pray. Eureka! You could pray. That was a confessional, a modern one. No religion, no affiliation was needed. Sure, agnostics and atheists were admitted as well. Anyone could confess whatever they liked and all would be forgiven, I swear, once you accepted the cold kiss of stone and a bit of transient, short-term decapitation.

Maybe not. This is my last guess. The thing was a dream machine. Yes, and yes! If you came at the crack of dawn, sacrificing breakfast, foregoing makeup... if you dove headfirst in the wall without reticence you could resume your dream, whatever it was. Follow it to its end, get the best of it rather than a few random scraps.

Some of us do care for conclusions.

Of course, you couldn't stay there indefinitely. It was not your private spot. It was a public commodity. If someone was in line you had to quit after a given time. Twenty minutes? Five, ten at most. After all there was a risk of asphyxia, and a slight one of madness. You need to see the light, breath fresh air at regular intervals.

Was the statue dreaming? I bet.

Was he, truly? The man with the briefcase? Didn't the attaché mean indeed that he was a doctor, a great psychoanalyst, scholarly trained to observe, study and brilliantly unscramble dreams? All of them, the entire town's, correct.

Well, this seems to be a sound interpretation... or else another dream, where the early hours belong even when you are walking.

Sleepwalking.

≈≈≈☼≈≈≈

AUGUR

The only change she perceived were the magpies. A pair... black and white so sharply contrasted on their plumage, she asked herself if the edges of those different patches bristled and burned, sending out electric waves as they touched, scorched like naked nervous ends. Black and white so bluntly interlocked, they hurt her eyes.

The only change she later recalled were the magpies.

But it might have been a false memory. Perhaps, only the turtledoves were around. The usual bunch, though since the sumac trees had been cut they had multiplied. Now, as soon as she stepped out to the yard, a whole flock took flight with a rustling, rippling sound of reverse waterfall.

Turtledoves... their increased crowd was a change, correct. On the minor side.

And that underwing tinge of blue? Not sure where exactly... a flash, very intense but hard to locate. Streak of periwinkle on brown. She hadn't seen it before. Was it new?

The scrub jay had changed as well. Lately, a fresh specimen had replaced the old one. She had nonchalantly accepted the switch, careless about the previous bird's fate. Change is cruel, that way.

The new scrub jay was plump and full-feathered, its plumage so glossy it looked false. But a joy to behold compared to the scrawniness of its predecessor. Bold, aggressive. As she packed, it landed on a windowsill and started hitting a pot with its beak, so near to the glass she feared it would magically cross it, seamlessly materializing inside.

It stubbornly tapped against cold aluminum, unabashed by her obtrusive closeness and exhibiting none of the well-known shyness of avians. She was tempted to fetch a few peanuts, lone remain in a stark naked kitchen, survived without a reason. Slide the window wide open, offer them on her palm. The jay would promptly accept the invitation, she knew. But the house had to be vacated, and she had no spare time.

≈≈◊≈≈

Still, those "dove" and "jay" modifications were somehow, she sensed, part of an organic cycle. The only worthwhile discrepancy were the magpies, if she hadn't merely imagined them. She could have. But the clashing tones of their plumage had left almost a crease on her corneas, a wound.

And what did the pies want? They must be attracted, like thieves, by the bric-a-brac, the odds and ends that inevitably fall behind, slip aside during transitions. They'd find the bits and pieces she'd later seek in vain, and weave them within the walls of their nest. Well, she should be glad! A good omen.

Unneeded.

She did not look for signs. No direction had to be pointed at. Wheels of fortune simply follow their course. No action on her side was required, besides clearing the place.

But she knew from precedent revolutions that in times of change details disappear... magpie booty. Details meaning things small, and yet precious. She recalled when, years before, cleaning the same home on arrival, she had dug a brooch out of a crack in the wooden floor (a deep crack, filled with dust so old it had calcified).

Surely lost by a previous tenant, it was quite old-fashioned. Oval-shaped, with large pearls cast in silver, in the art-deco style her mom favored. Wait! Wasn't it identical to a brooch her mother had owned, decades and miles away? If she shut her eyes she could see the alias (the original) pinned to the silk foulard Mother wrapped around her neck in cold weather. She recalled how she greedily pocketed her welcome gift.

Details are lost and found in times of transition. There are cons. There are pros. She could count on both. Now for instance, while packing, she retrieved a tool she had mislaid while scoring the bathroom's tiles. As she wanted them to be pristine for the next inhabitant, she had picked a long, tapered scalpel, tip a bit bent from usage and yet very sharp, very slim. Tool of choice, irreplaceable, it worked well in the thinnest interstices. At the end of the day she found it no more.

≈≈◊≈≈

But on leaving she did. In chaos, things get misplaced. Lost, found.

That tool was already missing a part, since time immemorial. Smart and handy, it sported two points for different purposes, one at each end... But one of them had fallen, so far back she couldn't remember its shape. She tried once on a while, by mere curiosity, but her memory unfailingly blanked. She was slightly dismayed...

Like when, still in a time of change, time of chaos, she had lost an angel card. Angel tarot. Very small, alas. Tiny figurine from a miniature deck employed to tell fortunes.

By then, she was prone to seek omens when life took brisk turns. When things got very instable she carried her deck in her purse. Once, she had drawn a card in the street, while she waited for something, for someone. Why so impellent? She had pulled just one card, placed it on the trunk of her car, turned it face up. Breathed in.

On the same night, at home, she had realized the deck was incomplete. Verify, please. Again. Minus one. Then, the card she had drawn earlier, outside, must be gone. Maybe her date had suddenly arrived, or had not and she had hastily left. A split second. Card fell on concrete. Her tires ran it over, perhaps.

That night, she hadn't been able to figure out which was missing. She had spread out the rest of the deck, to no avail. The angels were named after qualities, virtues. Good things. Say meekness, for instance. Say relief. Say courage, for instance. Say love.

She had not memorized them. She couldn't remember them all.

But she knew that she had drawn the card in the morning with her brother in mind. So the angel was, had something to do with, her brother. Now she feared she might have damaged her bro, pruning him off the deck. Panic punctured her like an insect sting, like an arrow. But her fright, of course, was immaterial and she got used to the maimed deck.

Worries about her brother soon faded. Though she lost her brother, it's true. Afterwards, her brother suddenly passed but, see, not the brother whose angel she had dropped during a time of change, revolution. That one remained unscathed. The other passed. The other brother.

≈≈≈☼≈≈≈

THE FLOWERS

Throughout the long wait for the police, then the invasion of fingerprints agents, they were in the vase but I didn't see them. My gaze was automatically drawn to the chaos, the destruction. The house looked like a bombed town. All that I could feel was a feverish urge of repair, made more painful by the forced delay. Only when everything was cleaned up I spotted them, and they struck me like a snapshot from another time. No, they didn't belong. They reflected a carefree, trustful soul that I no more owned.

Flowers mark nice occasions, don't they? Weddings, birthdays and such. They do not belong to catastrophe if not afterwards, maybe, to honor the dead. After the repeated gang threats, the robbery and vandalizing, I knew that I had to abandon the place, find a safe abode. Hastily, I threw my residual stuff into boxes, but I didn't dare touching the vase. The bunch both irritated and moved me… a strange combination of feelings. It moved me with a memory of time calm and peaceful, when its smile was appropriate. It hurt me by recalling how briskly that season was gone.

More than all, I was puzzled by the flowers' apparent naivety. It seemed as they had seen nothing. Could they have witnessed the brutality, a few inches from those angry hands, without any trouble? Didn't the thieves' motions and mugs leave a trace on those timid blossoms, frail stems, tender blooms? Did they realize danger? They must have. They would have called for help, I am sure, if they had known how. They would have alerted me, if…

Do plants have a soul? I bet. I think they are aware of who cares for them. They are responsive, somehow. Perhaps this is why the flowers kept silent, didn't budge, didn't blink. They played dead to avoid massacre. They made themselves small, inconspicuous, wishing to be there for me in the aftermath. To say, "Mom, we didn't run! Mom, we waited… Don't cry! Mom?"

I'd still like to toss these flowers. I will not, until the last minute. They did not betray me. They did nothing bad. They survived.

≈≈≈☼≈≈≈

THE FOUNTAIN

"As long as they don't murder you," he said under his breath, his gaze turning away from me while his gestures grew faster, more rhythmic. He was coiling a rope around a bundle of twigs, tying it with an expert knot, and his gestures took hold of him. They took the lead. Then his eyes went to the cabin door, and I shivered. He must be about to head inside, store that wood somewhere, perhaps pile it by the fireplace.

Was there one such? Was it just a hole in the floor? What was the floor made of? Dirt? I thought so. The fireplace must have been a dirt hole inside a dirt hole, so to speak, for what else was the cabin? A grotto, a cavern would have been better definitions. Although probably it wasn't dug into the mountain, in the twilight it looked like little more than an anthill. Were the walls made of mud? Mixed with rocks, gravel, branches? Not sure, but I hadn't watched very carefully.

My attention had been magnetized by his body, his face, the sound of his voice, and subliminally by the things he said... which I had heard, but they'd surface later. On the spot they didn't strike me as their owner did. Owner? Porter, carrier, I guess. If I had listened in casual fashion, more absorbed by his presence than by his words, the surroundings had registered even less.

Yes, I knew the cabin was there. I had acknowledged it as the place where he'd disappear at some point, but now it jumped to the foreground and looked dooming, imposing. His quick stare caused it to swell as if we were in Wonderland, and reality could whimsically shrink or expand. I was Alice. Who was he? No one... The whole metaphor was a useless diversion.

He would pass through that door and vanish. Chances to see him again were about nil.

And so what? After all I had known him for less than an hour. Not enough time to fall in love. Besides, he must have been as old as my grandpa.

Yes, I knew he was remarkably fit, though I couldn't truly see his body, bunched up in too large and too many rags. But I could feel the ease, the aplomb. See, he had chopped wood during our entire conversation without losing breath. He could manage chopping and talking. He sure had good lungs, considering how thin was the mountain air.

He moved with coordination and grace, his center of gravity just where it belonged, still supported by strong, tonic muscles, still untwisted by arthritic joints or weakened bones. His exposed parts, hands, neck, feet, looked healthy and he had a nice tan.

Strangely, his hair was short. A neat, whitish flattop. Weird. A ponytail dangling down to his calves would have made more sense. But the crew-cut looked clean.

Very clean. Can you picture a fellow in rags looking fresh and ready, like an athlete before the race?

His eyes were of the handsomest blue, stuck into the folds of his skin like glass from a broken bottle. They looked fake, mismatched with the earthy tones of his clothes, of the ground, leaves, rocks, trunks... The sky? Sure, but the sky was up there, unreachable, and that somehow justified its incongruous shade. Also, its expanse diluted its color, made it lighter and paler.

Nothing justified those eyes. Nothing diluted them.

I had found him, now that I think about it, by a series of errors.

First, the naïve assumption that I could hike the trails of a foreign land with no maps, and I wouldn't get lost. If I look at my attitude from a distance (namely, from the age I've reached now) I'm appalled at my degree of insouciance.

Well, I was a relatively seasoned traveler. I hit the road whenever I had saved enough money through any little odd job. Bye! And I traveled my way to the next. That went on for years in a row, and I liked to punctuate my journeys with excursions and hikes, simply following my whim. I recall starting on the trails with no plan at all, just leaving my tent or my room as soon as I woke. Out we go.

That day I had eaten a solid breakfast, I'm sure, as required by my young appetite. Bread and something, perhaps bread and bread. You can always find some and it fills you up. That plain, substantial meal would suffice me. You got it... I never brought lunch or snacks. Yes, I'd feel hungry sooner or later, and that time would be called "return." On my way back I'd be very or else incredibly hungry, depending on how long my strolling had been. None of those nuances worried me.

I did not carry water. Why bother? What is strange at being thirsty? When you get home, you drink.

My shoes for the hike were those I was wearing. I owned one pair until they fell apart and couldn't be fixed. Then I'd buy another pair. And I didn't choose proper clothing... I just grabbed what felt good at the moment. Later, when the sun would be high, I would knot my sweater around my waist.

Sure, I was often cold, not having considered winds, clouds, possible rain, altitude. I remember being unbearably cold and still bearing it, in the dumbest of way, just enduring. Then, whenever I'd take a warm shower or tuck in some bed I savored delightful relief.

I never fell sick. Don't ask why. Therefore I didn't learn from experience, being apparently impervious to its lessons. For decades I learned nothing. Neither carefulness, nor the need for planning. Neither caution, nor fear.

As for orientation... how clumsily did I manage those hikes! Night always surprised me in the midst of some impromptu detour. Time to find my way back, was it? I would either figure it out, or it would figure itself. Things would make sense. I would recall landmarks or else retrace my steps by mere instinct. Should I not, someone would certainly help me... I didn't prospect the eventuality of true, complete wilderness.

What a blank slate I was! No vision of evil had yet tainted my mind. Unless I had wiped it off.

If my insouciant roving, that morning, blessed by warm autumn colors and impervious to all care, was one of the aforementioned errors, the other was related to language. I had been in the country for several months, time for an employment or two, and spoke the local idiom. But I didn't master nuances... such as nouns and verbs sounding the same, for example.

I am talking about the term "falls," which for me was a present tense, third person. I had no idea it could also be a noun's plural. I'd refer to waterfalls as cascades. I would call a snowfall an avalanche. See?

Down, where the trail... Truly, I had called it "road" in my ignorance, giving it the same sturdiness, same stability of a paved roman avenue. Roads do not get blurred, fishtail or just vanish. They are mighty reliable.

Where the road started I'd seen an old wooden sign, worn but still decipherable, which said "Hermit Falls." I had laughed... To me it sounded like a pun, like a jocular version of "Deer Crossing," though it used the present instead of the gerundive (I wasn't yet capable of appreciating such subtleties). Who on earth would have written it? Why? I had no clue, but that is the essence of traveling. You accept what you don't understand.

Without expecting hermits (by the way, did they still exist? Had they ever, or were they purely fictional?) to crash down the slopes for my amusement, I had briefly thought that I'd find a fresco somewhere, a cave painting, a hermit-themed landmark of sorts.

But I forgot all about it, mesmerized by the charm of gorgeous trees wrapped in golden leaves. Trees of such poise, such majesty, they almost seemed to be endowed with something human. Superhuman, I mean.

While I walked, the woods became thicker and the valley grew distant, remote. Silence soon embraced me, though silence, you know, is never such in a forest.

I must have hiked for hours. All at once, the trail started descending.

I heard the thumps behind my back but they didn't scare me. On the contrary, I was exhilarated with curiosity, ready for a bear cub… something heavy, judging by the type of noise. I turned, and I saw him.

Though his colors melted with those of the background, his fast progress quickly defined him. He came down the slope with small, rapid steps, focused, concentrated on his walk. A large bundle of twigs was under his arm. An axe hung from a rope tied around his waist.

Common sense would had said, "beware of a man with an axe, even more if no one else is around." A tall, sturdy man. Well, not if he's been patently cutting wood. I moved over to let him pass, met his eyes, and he smiled. His teeth weren't in the best of conditions. I followed at my own pace.

When I arrived to the clearing I first saw the hut and then him, chopping close by. He had put down his bundle and worked on a pile of logs, cutting them in small pieces. I don't know why I sat on a stump, a few feet away, and started watching him. He must have been aware of my presence, but he didn't say a word. That was fine. I just needed a rest.

Then he let go of his axe and he wiped his brow with his sleeve. Slowly, and his gesture struck me. I held my breath for a second, in wait, feeling as if a change of status had happened, as if he had mopped away something other than sweat. He turned towards me, said "hi" and briefly introduced himself.

Now to save my life I couldn't recall his name. Don't think I haven't tried. I have tried a million of times. There's strictly no way. I must have told him mine, though I don't recall doing it. Which, of course, doesn't matter at all.

Then he asked me where I came from, where I was directed. Small talk... by then I didn't know of such expression, which I would have mistaken for a pun... Anyway, I'm sure I candidly answered all questions, though I remember nothing except that he soon stopped talking, as if that basic collection of data had fully sufficed him.

Well, the exchange had been a tad brief to my taste... His name, please? Could he kindly repeat it? Perhaps spell it? Oh god, why can't I recall it? Help! I'd give anything...

What was he doing there? He laughed. What a question. He lived there, and he was preparing for winter because it was fall. Duh.

Lived there all year 'round? Sure.

Had he always? Oh, no. Since when he had become a hermit, and he wasn't born one...

That seemed evident, in spite of my complete ignorance on the subject. I could guess it wasn't a thing you'd inherit like money, like genes. Still, how would you…

You'd choose at some point, he explained.

Out of the blue? (Why did I pick an idiom that I hardly understood? His eyes, maybe…)

Not truly. Rather, step by step. First he was a monk, with his brothers, in a monastery downhill. Meanwhile, he pressed his palms against the sides of his trousers. He grabbed his axe again.

Didn't he like it there? Yes, but he knew he would like it better up here.

Didn't he miss his mates?

His smile widened. Not like that of the Cheshire cat, not that kind of smile. His smile widened and it was like a secret garden. Like something I desperately wanted to get in, a kid grasping at a gate.

He smiled large and he didn't answer. He looked down and chopped harder. He did that, now and then. Looked away, chopped harder.

"Don't you care for people?" I insisted.

He kept quiet and I was at loss for a second, not knowing what to do with our chat. Should I drop it?

But the delayed answer came, "course I do." As banal as that.

Did he lie? Something made me think that he never did. Maybe he was forbidden. That is why he took his time replying… because he didn't lie.

"Do you see many people?" Another smile. "No one wanders around here." How come? I just got there, following a wooden sign.

"It's not much of a traveled trail."

He focused back on his task.

Later. "There's a monk who periodically visits. He comes checking on me. My health, mostly. And he brings a few things I need."

"Food?" escaped from my mouth.

"I don't need it. I can grow food. I have a little patch over there. Not much thrives, but some veggies do. He brings things I can't make out of thin air, candles, soap..."

Candles, soap and what else? He didn't reply. Maybe candles and soap.

As for clothing, what he sported seemed quite seasoned. Was he wearing that stuff when he first arrived? I mentally enlarged the checklist without need for him to confirm it. Needles, thread. Maybe just one needle. I was sure that he wouldn't lose it. By the way, you can fix clothes and shoes without needles. It is doable, I swear.

How often did his fellow monk visit? What did periodical mean? Now my question was worried. I had grown alarmed for reasons I couldn't detect. Probably I didn't know I was alarmed.

"Oh," he said, "when the season changes... every three months or so if weather permits. Last time he didn't come. August storms were terrible."

What if he didn't come? My worry was kind of swelling. Why?

He just smiled. I sensed he didn't want to reply. My questions weren't only naïve. They were stupid.

"You know…" he said. No, he couldn't have said such thing. "That is mostly for them," he said. "To make sure I'm fine. Not for me but for them." "They must know when they have to replace me," he added after a pause. Replace him?

"Don't you miss talking with people?" I asked.

I was feeling a creeping sadness. Oh, the subtlest of things. Creeping, subtle, like one of those little snakes Grandpa showed me when I was a child. Those he pointed at to teach me what a snake was, to acquaint me with them and hence prevent fear. Those snakes qualified for the job, though barely longer than worms. You would not want to touch them, of course (and they wouldn't let you), but you couldn't be frightened, no way.

Sadness (just a blade of it) crept on me like a snake so small, so irrelevant it could be called domestic… a pet.

Again, he wiped his brow. Again, slowly. He had put his axe down but didn't look tired. He wasn't. He might have decided I deserved a bit of attention, maybe in order to come to a conclusion, to get rid of me at last.

As he watched me, the weird sensation reoccurred. I felt like a… four-year-old? No. No more than three. Only two, and I can't go further back because that's when memory starts. A two or maximum three-year-old grabbing at the gate, those black iron bars, clutching them with my fists so strongly I could shake them.

I could pull them apart, I'm sure. I have such power in my arms, my palms, my ten fingers. I can feel it. I have all it takes, and yet it doesn't work. You know what? In fact I don't have to pull on those bars… I'm so small I could slip through. But it doesn't come to mind.

I was my young self, stuck outside the gate, drooling for the place I wanted to be in. Or else I was inside and the place was out. Would it matter?

"I can talk one hour per day," he said. "I have a whole hour."

Every twenty-four? Sure, that is what he meant. Quite an awful lot… Wait! Had I started reading his mind? Well, one hour seemed lavish and quite uselessly so. A waste, especially when nobody was there.

What did he do in that hour when he was by himself? He did not bother answering. Obviously the talking time wasn't a hygienic routine, something he had to perform in order to maintain sanity. One would think so, but no. He didn't have to talk to the elements, to the birds or squirrels or mice, to exercise his tongue.

The rule simply meant that in case of visitors all he was allowed was an hour. It set a limit, a boundary, as if with more exposure he could get contagion, I guessed. He could get infected, his immune defenses having meanwhile crucially dropped.

But what was I thinking? His defenses from what?

I had started understanding. Maybe just empathizing, with no reason involved. I was feeling what he might, must have felt.

Sure, one hour could be dangerously overwhelming once you had lost the habit. All that communicating could be inebriating and not in a good way. Listening to the nonsense could be sickening, nauseating.

Now it was quite obvious, for instance, that I had just talked nonsense. All my questions, what was he doing here, why, did he miss people, weren't they self-explanatory? Come on. Why did I ask things I myself could answer? Small talk. I didn't yet know the definition. That does not justify me.

It was sadness that made me talk, pushing up the next trivia.

Because sadness had widened a bit. Not to the size of a dangerous snake. Not yet.

(By the way there weren't many dangerous snakes, Grandpa said. Almost none of them. Size didn't matter. Even those so long they spread across the path, like a wavering bridge I had to overcome, were pacific. Even those thick as a shovel handle should not preoccupy me. They lived their life. They were loners. They didn't want to acquaint me. They detested interacting. They were scared of me, believe it or not. I should stay put, let them pass, be quiet, make no noise. They would not harm me if they didn't feel attacked. No! I could befriend snakes if I kept my distance. The only ones I should fear were vipers, those short fellows with bifurcated tongues, very easy to spot. Even they were okay though, if I left them alone.)

But enough of snakes!

Sadness had grown thicker and spoke through my tongue. Didn't he like people at all? Did he hate people? As if his previous statements had not quite registered, as if I were in dire need of reassurance.

That he might have guessed, for he replied with the largest of smiles, the most handsome I'd be graced with, that night, but I didn't know.

"I love people," he said. "I pray for them daily."

For an hour a day? I asked, almost thoughtlessly. Ha ha!

"I pray as many hours as I have left when I'm finished working. I don't count them," he said.

Then I asked another set of futilities to which he replied more and more courteously. More convivially, I'd say if such word made sense in that context.

As I said, I was aware of the fact that my inquiries were tautological. I asked mere variations of things I had already asked. I knew, and it dawned on me the clock had been ticking since when we had begun... Did his first nod count?

Did the hour start whenever he wished? Or had I arrived by chance at the canonic time, just before sunset? Both a classic (because kind of obvious) and a romantic choice (the forest in twilight).

Time in any case was going by. Though I couldn't tell how long the conversation had lasted, instinct said it would end soon.

And that terrified me. Was I in love? Please, you must be kidding. Of course not. But see, this had never happened before... I apprehended the idea of being kicked out, perhaps cut at mid sentence, because my interlocutor was done. I just dreaded the moment of my dismissal. I guessed it would be plain awful.

How naïve of me to ignore that I had endured, oh yes, plenty of times, the thing that so scared me! People seldom give you a whole hour of attention. Do they ever? They shut you off much sooner, close the door, lock you out without explanations.

Didn't I know? Didn't such truth register just because it wasn't openly expressed?

I only knew I didn't want that hour to end. Since it would, I didn't want to waste any second. I should ask questions, try to get answers, and I would hear him talk, which is what I craved.

I urged him to describe what his routine was.

Simply keeping alive! He hunted a bit, small rodents and birds that he roasted. The older he became, the less meat he needed. He collected berries, wild fruit, nuts of various kinds. He grew tubers and herbs. He gathered firewood. Winters were very long. He kept things in running order, the house, his clothes...

Clothes? In running order? All these tasks took time. Just enough. Plenty was left for prayer. Now, he said, the moment was coming.

What moment?

That was my dumbest one. And he didn't reply, but mumbled instead, "if they only could spare you, if you could..." I can't reproduce the exact wording.

Then he pushed the door. My chest fluttered as I expected him to be swallowed into his cave. But the impossible happened. He said I could come in. A few minutes were left, and he'd show me something.

Now you think the situation feels fishy. The plot finally thickens. You are wrong.

I do not remember much of the interior. It was dark and I began scanning the obscurity, prey of a morbid curiosity or of something else I cannot define. I looked for a fireplace, a stove... There was none. A desk? In a corner. Nothing on it, except for a wooden cross.

I looked for his bed but I couldn't find it. A blanket, probably an army one, lay along a wall. On the right, almost out of sight, another one hung like a curtain. He pulled it sideways and gestured me in.

I was struck by the glare. The luminosity.

Where did it come from? This wasn't a room. Maybe an alcove. A closet? A niche squeezed against the mountainside, almost roofless and therefore the sky was visible.

A source trickled down the rocky wall, as skinny as a snake and wavering likewise. The Hermit Falls were real, after all. The spring had its typical sound, fragile, chime like, and it seemed to emanate a flickering light, incongruously festive, as if it were sprinkled with sequins. That was the halo I had first noticed, a suffused, soft brilliance.

Where the drip hit the soil, it formed a sort of puddle. Tiny, with a verdant reflex. A cup was close by with no handle. Or a mug, or a bowl. I couldn't tell. It was very plain, the color of soil. But the firmness of its shape comforted me.

For a second the fountain (should I call it so?) mesmerized me. Its sight and sound fully absorbed me, as if the old iron gate had finally opened, without noise or resistance. Smoothly sliding, it had welcomed me in.

Then I turned his way. Oh my, he was on his knees, his head bent, and I panicked. He would talk no more.

I was wrong.

"Here I pray."

How I wanted him to say goodbye... I was eager for him to say I should go, get on the trail before dark, could he say that, please? I just needed to hear it. But I felt I had vanished from his mind. His lips moved, but no sound came out. He was murmuring incomprehensible words, as he had done when he had put his axe down, the first time, or when minutes ago he had reached for the door. The beginning, the end.

He was muttering things that perhaps I shouldn't... Should I? His eyes had rolled inward and backward, though they were still open. And they looked amazingly blue.

When I stepped out, night had fallen.

That's a common surprise in the woods... how abruptly the light fades after sunset. As I said, I wasn't the fearful type. The strange apprehension I had felt during the conversation (mostly, while I waited for the conversation to end) left me as soon as I began walking. A great calm took its place.

The road unwound under my feet as it always did, bringing me back to where I had started in the morning. I was hungry and thirsty, but I wasn't cold. My mood was quite excellent.

≈≈≈☼≈≈≈

PART OUT

I am preparing the old car for retirement. A ghost, engine on the verge of collapsing, the poor thing is no more worth repairs. If I stick to a given procedure, I am told, the government will take care of the spoils and provide a refund. Perfect. Perfect.

Following the required steps is lengthy and complex, but I'm neither losing courage nor seeking help, wanting to dispatch this business entirely on my own. Not sure why, all about it reminds me of a proper burial.

As I schedule mechanical checks and fill forms, I start clearing the vehicle of my belongings. Such a simple task compared to the rest! And yet it feels strange. I resist it.

I have experienced this with houses before. Who has not? The divesting of unanimated property is weird, vaguely obscene, a kind of reverse violation... Shouldn't we feel intrusive, aggressive, when we invade a neutral and virgin space (room, garden, or vehicle) with our messy insignia? It's the opposite that seems cruel to me. This undue subtraction, this abandonment of husks that have done nothing but shielding us, quietly meeting our needs.

I am not sentimental. I am pragmatic indeed, on the rough side. Still, I have to approach my unloading in gingerly fashion. Front seats. Back seats. Glove box, and then side pockets. Maps. CDs. Trunk, in various installments.

The keys aren't in my purse anymore. I rarely need them, hence I have stored them in a safe place, elsewhere. Fetching them is a little ritual each time, sort of "let's get ready to pay old auntie a visit." Sort of, "brace yourself..."

In the past I have parted with vehicles faster, selling them simultaneously to my new purchase, selling them for parts if in bad shape. Quickly and without regrets, in order to make room in my driveway.

This car isn't special. I suppose it has lingered just because I'm pursuing the bucks from the government instead than other options. That's all. But I have gone through the cleaning task slowly, with surprising reverence.

Respect, reverence... are these emotions? Not sure. I don't know what they are. I know where they lie. Deep. This really tastes like a burial.

Why am I so scared on delivery day?

I am afraid the engine might expire while I'll drive or else on location, right in front of the clerk to whom I should bring a quasi-dead-but-still-running item. The idea of having to tow the car home, burdened with the embarrassment of finding another disposal, appalls me, and I am nervous about the possible disappointment of not getting the money I have hoped for.

But I am just as wary of the opposite scenario... the car being accepted and my sudden carless status, if brief. Being far from home and having to find a lift.

My anxieties are pathetic, I know.

As I drive the car, possibly for the last time, I'm all ears, fearing that the engine might sputter, cough and then choke. I always listen to the engine, of course, but today its sound overwhelms me. It amazes me with its consistency, its power. It perplexes me and makes me dizzy.

Something in this noise exudes purpose and intent. It is... should I say coherent, contiguous? Synchronous, it works in solidarity. With me, I mean. With my heart, my breathing, my pulse. We are the same. Concerted. Concerned, are we?

The engine seems to be concerned about me, about safely bringing me where I am directed. Well, what a discovery! Wasn't it always the case? Perhaps not. Perhaps our alliance, our symbiosis before was simply mechanical. Then, why should things change when we are on the verge of splitting? Why now?

As I drive, I notice the sky and how porous it looks, bright with the extreme shine of those days when things memorable... Wait. Bright with the extreme, unbearable shine the sky sports whenever it likes, but I only notice on days when remarkable things occur, because those are the days when I notice things.

Today I'm noticing things. Pointedly the sky, how it burns, scorches and it's simultaneously cold.

All goes well. The engine duly behaves through the proceeding. Soon I will get a check, but not yet. Now we (car and I) are weighted on a scale. Then I am weighted alone. Then I am subtracted from the car, meaning the weight of my body is deducted from our combined

160

weight. Other things are performed, until finally I park where I am told, leaving the keys inside.

Afterwards, I call for a friend to give me a ride home and I sit in a sort of picnic area, like a kid waiting for mama in the schoolyard. Wind is blowing away a few clouds. The air is crisp.

Blue.

Which color? The clerk asked, among other questions. This one caught me unprepared.

The car?

Sure.

Blue.

The answer spilled out like a confession. It felt personal, as if we were speaking of eyes... And the question felt useless. If the car is going to be a cube of metal in minutes, does its color matter? It felt needless, the question, therefore inappropriate.

As I wait, the sky bothers me. Empty of clouds, it glares with the brash luminosity, oh yes, of those days when things remarkable happen. Things pivotal.

On those days I also notice people and places, though the most irritating, no doubt, is the atmosphere around and above me, poised with ineluctable vibes.

But I notice folks as they arrive to this spacious precinct, scanty built, sparse, agoraphobic, with its piles of crushed metal shimmering like waves in the background. I see people looking around in confusion, not sure where to go, paperwork fluttering in their hands like sails guiding their tentative route.

They get in and out of their vehicles as I have done an hour ago. Each of them has come to deliver four wheels, quite a trivial duty. Even so, because this is the last of something, everybody is cocooned, wrapped and haloed by a nuance of finality.

From my small metal bench I still see the car. Soon it will be lifted by one of those monster tractors, and wrecked. This is what I have brought it for. This is why I am paid. Which feels, let's admit it, like a Judas' deal.

Said without sentimentality, I swear. I know how to sort human from unanimated matter. I don't anthropomorphize. But you can be a Judas to non-sentient entities, and it is the same as it comes to qualify your doing. Mine, in this case.

I look at my car, unchanged, which I guess means innocent, orderly and obediently parked as always, in wait. Like a dog expecting its walk, my car waits to go places, to run. Engine, sound, heartbeat, rumble, pulse, guts, entrails, circulation... farewell.

Boy, this ignorance things are condemned to. This blunt unawareness. As if I, as if someone should let them know. This ignorance, fragile, makes a Judas of me.

Relax. Take it easy. Bye, blue car. I will linger on faux-feelings no more.

I have given to this old car a neat, proper burial and I have been paid in exchange. Shouldn't it feel good? A sort of inheritance... As if, not content of having served me so faithfully...

162

I detest the word "serve." Not content of having supplied unconditional solidarity, the car left me a present as well. A last hug. Last kiss.

Now the accountant to whom I ask if this sum qualifies as income explains that, because it is smaller than the price I initially paid, it's actually a loss. This is great for tax purposes but it doesn't correspond to reality, right?

This is a gain, I am sure. A gift, as I have said, for which I feel grateful. And embarrassed. Not sure if, not sure how I deserved it.

~~~☼~~~

AN ALPHABET OF BIRDS

Hawks don't come into the flats very often. They keep close to the mountains, favoring their verdant slopes, the foothills. They rarely visit this urban, too human area of town. But today, around lunchtime, I hear a mighty flapping of wings through the kitchen window. If the sound reaches inside, its cause must be remarkable. I dash out as fast as I can. Large birds fascinate me.

Look! A pair of hawks! Here is one, harsh and proud, descending askew, briskly twisting and then heading up high. The other? Gone. I have captured just a divarication, a fork creasing the air. But I'm sure that something has parted from the bird I am watching, an impression of dark, a double, a shadow, a ghost.

The two of them must have fought. Although it doesn't linger, the prevailing party remains in sight for a reason, as if to leave a mark or a signature, plant a flag. Savor victory, all right.

They have fought upon something, of course. There's a fluff of down in the grass. A small body must be lying somewhere, as I have seen none in the winner's claws. Unless I mistook winner and loser... did I?

In the evening, the scrub jay's song is irritatingly plaintive. Very unusual, it sounds like a lament. A short one. Jays aren't melodious. They can't easily whine. Their calls are brief, staccato. The scrub jay that lives around here is no exception, but tonight it keeps repeating its cry, as it comes close, with increasing frequency. Sort of, "mom... mom... help... help..." Well, what can I do? I just saw that its neck is badly plucked. It must have fought for life, battling a daunting pair of resolute hawks. And it won, with some collateral loss.

Luckily, feathers will grow back... Jays are vain and with reason, as when in good shape they look splendid. Now the lad is circling around me, probably venting its midday squabble with the predators it had the misfortune to meet. But no, in fact it doesn't mind me. It inspects its subterraneous safes, I mean the geography of nuts that it keeps buried in the yard, with a sort of anxiety, either verifying the attack didn't also imply looting, or else seeking to wrap up the eventful day binging on comfort food. Nuts, nuts, and more nuts.

I don't know how the scrub jay and the squirrel also domiciled in my yard sort their burial sites. That they wouldn't erroneously tap from each other's pantry seems utterly impossible. Their underground shelves intersect so tightly, they are so unmeshed, for what I can see, that I would go crazy. Kind of, "whose socks are in my T-shirt drawer?" or, "what are your cigs doing in my purse?" We are all familiar, somehow, with domestic chaos, or the burden of a messy roommate. But the squirrel and scrub know how to keep it straight. I haven't seen them quarrel, not once.

I am out here, beer in hand, unwinding, listening to the jay's sobs as I watch its dinner rituals, because I want to catch the last of sunset, the thin strip of pink at the horizon. But a noise distracts me, other than the jay's broken litany... a fast, frantic click of metallic nature. Once more, I look up. A hummingbird flutters as high as I didn't think it could rise. And I'm hearing the flapping of its wings while it hangs above me. I mean, it stays in place. Yes, afloat, so to speak, thanks to muscle power and joint flexibility. Why? What for? No colorful bush is in sight. Blooms have shut their doors by this time of day, plus the guy is going nowhere, as I said.

Like a minimal flag, reckless red, it keeps flapping and I am seized by a sense of urgency, as if the tiny being bore a crucial message, wished to warn me about an impending threat or instead ask for help, help, help (like the plaintive jay)... Oh, my. I would need a stronger drink to ponder the drama inherent to birds' life, something I hadn't noticed so far, today jumping at me with full evidence. I would need a much stronger drink and therefore I'll pass.

Anyhow, now the creature darts off as if nothing happened. And I feel reassured, of course. This is the main point, is it? Birds are relatively vulnerable, but thanks god they can fly. Such skill doesn't grant survival, and yet doubtlessly it hastens the denouement of a few nasty spots. I am reassured about the hummingbird's fate, but still pondering about the strange noise it made, robotic, mechanical, as if letting me know it was fake. Artificial, a toy, maybe an electronic device? Little recording camera or else micro-micro-phone... humming bird, are you real? So perfectly and yet so incongruously made, you suggest to take your flesh-and-bloodiness with a small grain of salt.

My beer having sufficiently unwound me, I am walking inside when a giant butterfly skims my cheek. Night is falling but I can still guess its color. No, it isn't a moth... it is the first swallowtail of the season, gracing me with its splendor. In twilight? The insect must be confused. Lost in space, time, or both. It is rushing somewhere with the flourishes, curves and figure eights meant to distract pursuers, dashing them with a pretend courting dance. Hurried, though, as if it were late for a party, which is what its attire suggests. Please go! I would if I were invited. Its wing meets my cheekbone like a pair of soft, gentle fingers saying, saying...

Today things repeat but also get smaller. The same, smaller and smaller. Like an inverted pyramid, its tip pointing down.

≈≈≈☼≈≈≈

THE VOLVO AND THE BIKE

The old Volvo with a scratch on the side, parked next to my car in the library lot, looks familiar. Haven't we met before? I should ask, as if it were an acquaintance whose name I can't recall. A forgotten part of myself?

Correct. Of my dream-self, a wish from my teen years... I planned on buying a car like this one, see, as soon as I'd grow up. Perhaps not right away, but almost.

Alas, for a long time I had no car at all. Being steadily broke, I walked miles and took buses. When things slightly improved, my car wasn't what I'd choose but what I could get, second hand, cheap bargain. That was true for everything I possessed, clothes, home, job... my partner as well, I suspect, and it worked just fine.

Therefore, the Volvo slipped out of my mind. When I thought of cars I just wished the one I drove would be immortal, of course. Only in moments of fleeting enthusiasm, of irrational hope, when I envisioned money and luck one day would befall me, did I recall the first object of my longing. Used, pre-owned, salvaged, all right. No matter how kinked or bumped, no matter which color. Sturdy engine. Strong Swedish parts. Spacious, stretched like a train, a boat. Oh my, the amount of stuff it could hold!

I suspect this was the very core of my passion. What initially sparked my feelings must have been the Volvo's capacity in such slim body. As I pictured myself at the wheel I smiled, thinking of what trunk and seats might contain.

Not a bunch of children... well, a few. Mostly equipment and artifacts. Paintings, sculptures. Easels, canopies. Music stands, amps and microphones... All the elements of my traveling trade, multifarious and marked by an abundance of cumbering props. They would fit in the Volvo together with roadmaps and food, raincoats, swimsuits, of course books and notebooks.

The car's magic proportions would allow yet another accomplishment. I'd be able to pick from the sidewalk all those relics I transmuted into art, stage décor or home furniture. No shelf case, no ripped Japanese shade would be left behind with nostalgia. There would be no limit to the size of my rescued Christmas trees, those I'd try to put back into the ground.

And the Volvo would give credibility to my career choices, would it? Making transportation proper and safe, it would justify my not-quite-orthodox lifestyle.

In the library lot, at once, I realize how the perspective has changed. My desire has shot down without me noticing. I can sense it while in front of its object... nothing lights up, nothing fires. Time has run out, I guess. Now I wouldn't be able to lift the goods I wished to stuff in. I no more crave early setting of market booths. I'm fed with performance. I do the same things with less enthusiasm, especially no expansionistic views.

On the contrary, my views have become reductionist. Not that I'd want to change. I have kept the same loves. I have deepened into them, in fact. Only, tiny concentrates are what I can stand. What I need now is lightness.

I have reached and surpassed the Volvo phase, though without the Volvo. I've carried a lot inside the cars I could afford. I've picked from the street as much as I could handle. I've done things and been places. I have exhibited and I've been exposed. I have been quite fulfilled... Maybe I didn't realize it. Maybe I felt it in portions, installments, unaware that the installments added up to the whole. I thought my finish line was ahead, while I was past the finish line.

I have taken the sweet path of return, wavering through the countryside, amazed at the beauty of wild flowers. What I dream about on this evening dusty road is to leave my last car for a bike. I know, it sounds as going back to the beginning. A bike...

Should I tell about the first one I rode without training wheels? An instant of panic, and Dad hit me, as he took my hesitation for cowardice without giving it more than five seconds of trial. As he slapped me, my lips hit the handle and I got a small cut. Unavoidably, blood makes emotions swell or collapse.

I gave up. Dad went for an afternoon nap while Mom, quietly, sent me to my room, where I mindlessly and mechanically started to bump my brow against the wall. I'll never forget that hour. I kept hitting concrete with my head, though I didn't and still don't know why. Was it weariness? Was it self-loathing? Wish to justify my dad's opinion of me?

170

I eventually stopped and went out in the torrid mid-august sun. Daddy slept. In a blink I hopped on my bike, concentrated and rode. Easy. I mastered it in minutes. What a thrill! I became a bike lover until my belated first car. I guess I shall soon return to that cheap, darling locomotion. To that skill earned with some loss and some glory. It should be my next goal, my new horizon.

Do I think I betrayed myself not getting the Volvo? The name sounds like "I want" in my native tongue. It has fragments of the word "revolution" in more than a language. Sure, I "wanted a revolution" in my teen age, and I promised I'd get it no matter how. Did I?

If yes, I didn't receive a mention about it. No degree, no diploma, not even the diplomatic vehicle, so to speak, I aspired to ride in. I was granted no hash mark for rebellious feats, or they were quite brittle, quite thin. They are crumbling, as I pedal away.

≈≈≈☼≈≈≈

GARDENER'S COMPANION

As my mind floats above, my body, underneath, bent, accordion-folded, performs its own rituals.

A tight pinch, a brisk yank, and I toss the weeds I just pulled into the trashcan, while the smell of green reaches my neurons like a familiar touch, a caress. Smell of green that is so disparate from the color, so un-fresh, thick and muddy. This smell, truly, is brown.

Now I breathe it in from my fingers, and identity snaps at me like a cool breeze sneaking under the sheets, like a pleasant chill waking me up. "This is I," say my nostrils, meaning, "I am you." I do what you always did, my fingers having held yours long enough to learn the trade by infusion, skin to skin.

When I almost unconsciously bend to manicure Mother Earth, grooming her as you did until your last day, with me tottering at your side (yes, you combed Mother Earth, beautifying it with small and decisive gestures as you might have dusted and swept the luxurious hall of a palace)...

When I gather my body in a fist, a jack-in-the-box ready to spring back, then ball up again to catch another parasite growth, I feel rooted, firmly attached to you, meaning to the past, to all who ever lived. And the scent that hems me, rims me and be-rings me is a lingering sweat of love I don't want to rinse, is the aftermath of an embrace I want to be indelible. It is a good humor. It's the secret that makes me sing.

172

ABOUT THE AUTHOR: TOTI O'BRIEN

TOTI O'BRIEN is the Italian Accordionist with the Irish last name. She was born in Rome, Italy, raised in Sicily and France. After touring Europe and Brazil with her itinerant theater, in the early nineties, she established herself in Los Angeles where she makes a living as a self-employed artist, performing musician and professional dancer. O'Brien's first book of stories, *Africa*, was published in 1990. It was followed by another short story collection, *Reversed Memories*, two illustrated children books and an essay collection, *Lanterna Magica,* gathering selected work out of her long-term collaboration with Italian journals and magazines. O'Brien started writing in the English language in 2004. Since then, her poetry, fiction and non-fiction were published in hundreds of journals and anthologies in the US, UK, Ireland, Canada, India, Australia, and all over the world. Her most recent appearances include *The Moth, The Hamilton Stone, The Los Angeles Review of Books,* and *World Literature Today.* Her poetry collection *Other Maidens* (BlazeVOX, 2020) is about to be released. Her work was nominated for Best of the Net, Best Small Fiction, Best American Essay, the Pushcart, and various other prizes. Her memoir 'Nicotine' won a nonfiction prose award in 2018. Her essay 'Blur In The Front Line' won the Anthony Award in 2016. Besides her creative writing, she contributes articles and reviews about art, music, film, literature and civilization to several magazines. She also translates poetry and prose from the Italian, the Spanish, and the French. O'Brien's multimedia artwork was exhibited in group and solo shows in Europe and the US, since the early nineties. Her paintings, sculptures, collages and textiles were featured in many publications, and she has produced book covers and illustrations.

≈≈≋☼≋≈≈

www.ingramcontent.com/pod-product-compliance
Lightning Source LLC
Chambersburg PA
CBHW051831090426
42736CB00011B/1750